I0460131

People Powered by AI

*A Playbook for HR Leaders Ready to Shape
the New World of Work*

Theresa Fesinstine

© 2025 by Theresa Fesinstine
Published by Culture Markers, LLC
https://www.peoplepower.ai
ISBNs:
Ebook: 979-8-9924175-0-0
Paperback: 979-8-9924175-1-7

All rights reserved. No part of this book may be reproduced, stored, or shared in any form without written permission from the publisher, except for brief excerpts used in reviews, articles, or educational settings as allowed by law.

Disclaimer: This book is for informational purposes only. While efforts were made to ensure accuracy, the author and publisher make no guarantees about completeness or results. Content is based on experience and research; outcomes may vary. Professional advice should be sought where appropriate. The author and publisher are not liable for any actions taken based on this material.

Trademarks: peoplepower.ai™ is a trademark of Culture Markers, LLC. Any other product names, company names, or trademarks mentioned in this book are the property of their respective owners.

Cover Design & Interior Layout: Theresa Fesinstine & Nick Fesinstine
First Edition: 2025

For Nick: *For his absolute support and encouragement. And for the silly dances that forever make me laugh. We are in this together.*

Robble, Robble.

Contents

Introduction
People First, AI Forward

For as long as I've been in HR, one thing has remained constant: the best workplaces are powered by people. Not policies. Not perks. Not even mission, vision, or values. It's people.

And yet, the role of an HR leader today is vastly different from when I first got started in the late '90s. Work is evolving fast, and Artificial Intelligence isn't just knocking on our office doors. It's already inside. It's transforming how we hire, engage, develop, and retain talent. Some frame AI as a threat to our humanity. Others treat it like a magic fix. The truth is somewhere in the middle. When used wisely, AI has the power to elevate our business and elevate us too.

Still, too many HR leaders are stuck reacting to AI-driven change instead of leading it. Often, they're left out of the conversation altogether. That's a problem, because no one understands people, culture, and ethics like HR does. And the reality I've uncovered through educating over 10,000 HR professionals is clear: the future of HR isn't about AI taking over. It's about HR professionals like you learning how to use AI to create workplaces that are more efficient, more strategic, and more human.

If AI feels overwhelming, especially if you're more comfortable with people than with technology, you're not alone. That's exactly why I wrote this book. To serve as your learning companion. To be the guide I wish I had when everything started accelerating. We're not here to get lost in jargon. We're here to figure out how AI can help you right now, in the real-world HR situations you face every day.

Imagine sitting down with a trusted friend. Someone who understands what you're going through because they've lived it. They're a few steps ahead and ready to share the tools, questions, and approaches that can help you see new possibilities. That's the kind of relationship I want this book to offer.

This isn't a tech-heavy textbook. It's a practical playbook filled with real-world examples, exercises, and templates you can actually use. You'll build prompts, assess tools, lead conversations, and design strategies that reflect the challenges you face in your organization. We'll cover the important topics like ethics, bias, data privacy, and change management, because leading with AI isn't just about knowing how to use it. It's about using it with intention and care.

Rather than asking "What can AI do?" the better question is "How can AI help us do what we do best with greater impact?"

You've probably tried out tools like ChatGPT or noticed new AI features in your HRIS. Maybe you've heard about predictive analytics improving retention strategies or used automation to save time. With those tools come new questions:

- How do we protect the human connection that's essential to HR?
- How do we ensure our use of AI is fair and inclusive?
- What do we need to know to lead our organizations?

I wrote this book to help HR Leaders answer these questions.

Over the past two years, I've worked with HR teams across industries, tested tools, built and refined prompts, and helped HR leaders integrate AI into their work in meaningful ways. That journey led to peoplepower.ai, an education and consulting company I founded to support HR leaders in understanding and using AI. My mission is to make AI accessible and actionable for those of us who lead with people in mind. This book is a reflection of that mission.

You'll find opportunities throughout these pages to experiment, reflect, build, and apply. This book was written to help you lead in your way, using your voice, and aligned with your values. The more you bring your experience into the process, the more this book will serve you.

By the end, you won't just understand how to use AI. You'll have the tools to lead with it. From rethinking recruitment to navigating ethics, you'll walk away with practical strategies and real confidence to create meaningful, people-centered change.

So let's take this step together. Whether you're looking to streamline your operations, design stronger learning experiences, or build your team's readiness for change, everything you need starts right here.

Let's dive in. It's time to lead.

Theresa

Author's Note

Shaped by Experience, Sharpened by AI.

Yes, I used AI to help write this book. Not to generate fluff, but to challenge my thinking, punch up my arguments, and clarify my message. Just like a writer uses an editor or a coach uses film review, I used AI as a tool.

The insights here are mine. The perspective is rooted in lived experience. But AI helped me pressure-test ideas, streamline complexity, and stay current.

If there's one thing I want you to take from this, it's this: the best results come when smart humans leverage smart tools. The future belongs to those who can collaborate with AI without losing their voice.

Chapter 1

AI Basics, No BS

What Every HR Leader Needs to Know

B efore we dive into real-world applications, we need to get grounded. This section will give you the essential foundation to understand AI clearly and speak about it confidently, even if you're not the most technical person in the room.

We'll start by exploring what AI really is, and what it isn't. We'll explore some common fears and misconceptions, helping you separate AI fact from fiction. You'll learn about the different types of AI, from rule-based systems to machine learning and deep learning, and understand how they relate to HR functions.

Don't worry—we won't get bogged down in technical jargon or complex algorithms. Instead, we'll focus on practical understanding. By the end of this section, you'll be able to:

- Explain AI concepts in simple terms to your colleagues and stakeholders
- Identify potential AI applications in your HR processes
- Understand the basic principles behind AI decision making
- Recognize the key considerations and limitations of AI systems

Remember, knowledge is power. By demystifying AI we're taking the first step towards leveraging its potential to transform our work and the organizations we build. So, let's pull back the curtain and get started.

1.1 What is AI? An HR Perspective

When you hear "Artificial Intelligence," what comes to mind?

If you think of robots taking over jobs or incomprehensible algorithms making decisions in the dark, you're not alone (and you're not exactly wrong...). But here we are, and AI is far more practical, accessible, and integrated into everyday tools than science fiction ever predicted.

Think of AI as a modern library not just filled with books and information, but organized to help you find, interpret, and create. In this analogy:

- **Machine Learning Models (MLMs)** are like the cataloging system, classifying information by topic and purpose, learning over time to improve how it sorts and prioritizes.
- **Large Language Models (LLMs)** are the stacks and collections themselves, huge repositories of information, context, and relationships that the system can draw from.
- **Natural Language Processing (NLP)** is the librarian, skilled at interpreting your question, finding what matters, and even adjusting tone or translating your intent.
- **Generative AI (GenAI)** is your personal research assistant that can help you synthesize sources, generate summaries, and even draft new content based on everything it's seen before.

And just like a great librarian, AI doesn't just retrieve information, it helps you understand what to do with it.

AI systems today go far beyond storing information. They surface patterns, make predictions, and guide decision-making in real time. For HR professionals, this means access to insights that were previously buried under spreadsheets, slow processes, or gut-based decision-making. These tools can quickly identify trends, forecast risks, and offer data-backed recommendations enabling HR to lead with speed and confidence.

In the same way, AI helps HR professionals navigate complexity through processing large volumes of data, recognizing patterns, and providing timely insights that support stronger, faster decision-making.

Here's how that translates in real HR work:

- **Pattern Recognition:** AI can scan thousands of data points to detect trends in engagement, hiring, turnover, or performance Insights that might take months to surface manually.
- **Prediction:** Based on historical data, AI can forecast who might be at risk of leaving, or which new hire is most likely to succeed.
- **Decision Support:** Whether it's choosing candidates, customizing L&D paths, or optimizing your comp strategy, AI helps you make faster, smarter decisions by turning data into actionable insights.

Remember, AI in HR isn't about replacing the "human". It's about augmenting our capabilities, allowing us to work smarter. As we progress through this book you'll see how AI can be a powerful ally in creating more effective, efficient and empathetic HR practices.

Now that we've built a clear, intuitive understanding of what AI *feels like*, aka how it operates like a modern library, let's ground that insight in more technical terms. In the next section, we'll walk through the primary types of AI systems used in business today, and how each one plays a role in the HR ecosystem.

Exercise:
AI in Your HR World

Throughout this book, you'll find exercises designed to help you think critically, apply concepts immediately, and track your evolving perspective. Consider this your working space. A living journal to accompany your learning as you go through each chapter and subsection.

To get started, open a blank document, grab a notebook you'll use consistently, or feel free to write directly in these pages. For this first reflection, take a moment to think about your current HR workflows.

1. Where do you and your team spend time on repetitive tasks?

2. Where are decisions made without enough data?

3. Where could more personalization or prediction improve the employee experience?

Consider three areas where AI, based on what we've just covered, could support or improve your work. Don't worry about tools or implementation just yet. We'll revisit these ideas as we move deeper into AI's role in the employee lifecycle.

1.2 How AI Actually Works... Without the Hype

Let's take the conceptual model from Section 1.1 and translate it into how AI is actually built and categorized in the real world. These classifications will help you evaluate tools, talk to vendors, and explain your choices to technical and non-technical stakeholders alike.

Now that you've got the big picture, let's translate the library metaphor into the technical categories that shape how AI is built and used. These classifications will help you better evaluate tools, lead cross-functional conversations, and anticipate the strengths and limitations of different systems.

In this section, we'll go beyond quick definitions to break down how each type of AI functions, what it means for HR, and what you need to watch out for when evaluating these technologies.

Rule-Based Systems—These follow strict, predefined rules. You can think of them as "if-then" logic machines. They don't learn, evolve, or adapt; they just execute the conditions they're given.

- In HR, these systems are commonly used for tasks like resume screening, initial eligibility checks, or automated email routing. They're useful for straightforward, high-volume decisions, but lack nuance or contextual understanding.

- *Example: An applicant tracking system (ATS) that automatically filters out resumes without specific keywords or a required number of years of experience, without considering transferable skills or potential.*

Machine Learning (ML)—ML systems learn by identifying patterns in historical data and applying those patterns to future decisions. They adapt over time, improving as they're exposed to more data and feedback.

- In HR, this can mean analyzing past hiring data to determine which candidates are most likely to succeed, or evaluating engagement data to predict which teams may struggle with burnout.
- *Example: A recruitment tool that learns from your top-performing hires and adjusts its recommendations to surface applicants with similar profiles, even if they don't match traditional resume filters.*

Deep Learning—A subset of ML designed for working with large volumes of complex, unstructured data such as images, video, audio, and open text. Deep learning systems often power some of the most advanced AI applications.

- In HR, this shows up in tools that can analyze video interviews, extract sentiment and behavior insights, or evaluate voice tone and body language cues in leadership coaching scenarios.

- *Example: A system that scores candidate interview recordings based on subtle communication cues, like confidence, clarity, and adaptability.*

Natural Language Processing (NLP) —NLP allows AI systems to understand, interpret, and generate human language. It can extract meaning from messy, unstructured text, including nuance, tone, and even implied intent.

- In HR, NLP powers tools like sentiment analysis of employee feedback, resume parsers, or chatbots that help with policy questions and onboarding support.
- *Example: A chatbot that helps new managers role-play tough conversations by generating realistic employee responses, guiding them with coaching prompts in real time.*

Generative AI (GenAI)—These systems can create original content like text, images, video, and more, based on patterns learned from massive datasets. They're what power tools like ChatGPT, DALL·E, and other AI content generators.

- In HR, GenAI can draft job descriptions, build personalized development plans, write learning materials, or help employees self-serve answers from policy documents.

- *Example: An HR business partner using ChatGPT to create a tailored onboarding schedule for a new sales hire, incorporating role-specific content, introductions, and deadlines.*

Predictive Analytics—This approach uses data patterns to forecast likely outcomes. It doesn't generate new content, but it helps anticipate what's coming next, and what to do about it.

- In HR, predictive analytics is central to workforce planning, turnover forecasting, and internal mobility. The key is turning insight into action.
- *Example: A dashboard that predicts which high-performers are at risk of leaving and recommends tailored interventions like stretch projects or retention bonuses.*

Remember, in practice, many AI solutions in HR will combine several of these approaches. You don't need to master the math... you just need to recognize what they're doing so you can ask the right questions and lead strategically.

Exercise:
AI Types in Your HR Toolkit
Think about your current HR processes. Can you identify where each type of AI might be beneficial? For instance:

1. Where does your team already use rule-based systems to simplify a repetitive task?

2. How might machine learning improve your decision making over time?

3. Where could NLP enhance communication with employees or candidates?

By understanding these different types of AI, you're better equipped to identify opportunities for AI integration in your HR practices and to have informed discussions with vendors or IT teams about AI solutions. In fact, you may find yourself in a position to educate them!

1.3 Truthtelling the Biggest Fears About AI

Even with a solid understanding of what AI is and how it works, HR leaders and employees alike are still wrestling with a range of fears, some rooted in experience, others in uncertainty. These concerns can stall progress, erode trust, and prevent meaningful adoption if they're not proactively addressed.

Let's walk through 10 common fears about AI, and unpack the reality behind each one.

1. Fear: *AI will eliminate jobs across HR teams.*

   Reality: We called this chapter *No BS* for a reason, so

I'm not going to start now. AI will replace some jobs, transform others, and leave a few untouched. Yes, it will automate plenty of routine work. But here's the flip side: it also creates space for HR to step into more strategic, high-impact roles. The work that centers on culture, ethics, innovation, and change management? That's about to become even more valuable.

Rather than eliminating HR, AI expands the function's potential if we adapt with intention and lead the transition thoughtfully in workforce planning, ethics, and transformation. This is our moment to focus on the runway ahead, not just for HR, but for our organizations as a whole. That means prioritizing upskilling, reskilling, and *new skilling* individuals, and reimagining how HR delivers value at every level.

2. Fear: *AI is too complex for non-technical professionals to understand or use.*

Reality: AI fluency doesn't require technical expertise. it requires curiosity, critical thinking, and the ability to ask better questions. A new job of HR leaders will be to bridge people and technology. That means understanding the goals of the tools, evaluating risk, and championing outcomes that support people, not just processes. You need to understand the logic. Many tools are designed for business users, and your job is to ask smart questions, assess risk, and connect tech to outcomes. That's leadership, not engineering.

3. Fear: *AI is biased.*

Reality: AI can reflect and even magnify systemic inequities if the data it learns from is flawed. Understanding how models are trained, tested, and governed is key to using them responsibly. HR must play an active role in bias audits, model evaluation, and pushing vendors for transparency and explainability. AI can inherit and amplify patterns in flawed data, making oversight more important, not less. Tools are only as fair as the teams and systems that build and monitor them.

4. Fear: *AI can fix culture or engagement issues.*

Reality: AI can surface valuable insights like disengagement trends or team sentiment shifts, but it can't lead, listen, or rebuild trust. Tools can augment your ability to diagnose issues, but healing culture requires leadership, communication, and emotional intelligence that only humans provide. It can help you diagnose what's happening, identify hotspots, sentiment shifts, or risky trends, but it can't rebuild broken trust or poor leadership. That still takes people.

5. Fear: *AI is a single tool or platform.*

Reality: AI includes a range of technologies and tools, such as Machine Learning, Natural Language Processing, Predictive Analytics, and GenAI. Each has unique use cases and risks. Knowing the difference empowers HR to ask the right questions and build stronger partnerships with Data and IT colleagues and vendor partners.. Natural language tools do one thing. Predictive models another. GenAI is something else entirely. Understanding these building blocks helps you make smarter vendor decisions and avoid black-box thinking.

6. Fear: *Only large or tech-savvy companies can benefit from AI.*

Reality: AI doesn't require a massive budget or a dedicated data science team. Many cloud-based tools are designed for mid-sized or resource-constrained teams. What's needed is a willingness to pilot, iterate, and lead with purpose, experiment more freely, and integrate tools without bureaucracy. The barrier is less about size and more about mindset.

7. Fear: *You need perfect data to get started.*

Reality: There's nothing more humbling than to be confronted with a new system implementation and see the lack of structure and consistency in your data once it is jumbled in a your new (expensive) system. With AI you don't need spotless data, you need useful data and a clear problem to solve. Many AI tools are designed to work with imperfect or messy inputs. Start with what you have, and make data quality part of your AI learning curve, not a barrier to entry. Many tools can work with what you already have and get smarter over time.

8. Fear: *AI will erode human connection.*

Reality: When AI is used to reduce busywork, leaders gain time for what really matters: coaching, culture-building, and connecting with people. The more we automate the transactional, the more room we create for transformational leadership. When it's used to remove administrative burden, HR has more time to coach, connect, and care for people. That's the opportunity.

9. Fear: *AI adoption means loss of transparency and control.*

Reality: Clear governance builds trust. HR should lead the way in defining ethical standards, requiring explain-ability from vendors, and ensuring employees under-stand how AI impacts decisions. Openness isn't optional... It's the foundation of responsible AI.

10. Fear: *Using AI means invading privacy or surveilling employees.*

Reality: AI can be used for good or for harm, it just depends on how it's deployed. Transparency, consent, and boundaries are non-negotiables. Ethical AI in HR requires safeguards, communication, and accountability at every level of design and use. Ethical HR teams put consent, clarity, and purpose first. That's how you use data responsibly and earn employee trust.

Understanding these fears is step one. Proactively addressing them is where HR leadership begins. These are the conversations that earn trust, unlock innovation, and ensure AI adoption strengthens your culture.

Exercise:
From Fear to Forward Motion

You've just unpacked the most common fears HR leaders and employees face around AI. Now it's your turn. Take 10 minutes to reflect on the following:

1. Which fear resonated most with you, and why?

2. What conversations have (or haven't) happened about this in your organization?

3. What could *you* do to lead or shape that conversation?

Use this reflection to start mapping your role not just as an adopter of AI, but as a translator, coach, and culture guide. We'll build on this in the coming chapters.

You've now built a foundation of knowledge, strategy, and emotional readiness. You understand what AI is, how it works, and what it means for your role in HR.

Next, we move from concept to execution, examining how AI is already showing up across the employee functions. This is where the theory becomes real.

Chapter 2

From Buzz to Business
Real AI Use Cases in HR

I t's time to roll up our sleeves and dive into how it's actually being used in HR today. In all my years in HR leadership, the changes I've witnessed recently with AI are unlike anything I've seen before. It's exciting, slightly overwhelming, but mostly full of potential.

In this section we're going to explore applications through the lens of the employee lifecycle, seeing firsthand how AI is reshaping everything from talent acquisition to employee engagement.

Here's what you can expect in the coming pages:

- Real world examples of AI in action: We'll look at concrete cases of how AI is solving HR challenges.

- Interactive exercises: In my experience, the best way to learn is by doing. I've included some activities to help you envision how AI could work in your own HR processes.
- Honest discussions about AI's limitations: As much as I'm excited about AI's potential, I'm a realistic optimist. There are hurdles and challenges and we'll talk candidly about where AI shines and where it falls short.

By the time we wrap up this section you'll be able to:

- Spot opportunities in your HR processes where AI could make an immediate impact
- Understand the pros and cons of implementing AI in different HR functions
- Articulate to your leadership team how AI can boost HR's strategic value
- Start brainstorming AI driven initiatives for your own department

Let me share a quick personal story. When I started exploring AI in December 2022, I was blown away. Suddenly, I was creating business docs and brainstorming ideas that used to take hours or a legal advisor. I was hooked.

And the more I used it, the more I found myself reflecting on all the processes and tasks that used to take forever, or felt emotionally exhausting. The ones where I'd sit, stuck, trying to find the right words. I kept thinking: *where was this tool when I needed it most? (Covid anyone?)*

But then I got curious: how could these tools help HR teams? How would HR teams feel about using them? Would they be excited too, or stuck in the usual Ego vs. Legal tug-of-war?

Early in 2023, most HR leaders I spoke with hadn't even heard of tools like ChatGPT. But as we moved closer to 2024, as awareness grew, so did their interest, alongside a mix of overwhelm and intimidation from all the tech jargon. What was needed wasn't just a demo, they needed someone who spoke their language and understood their world. Someone that has been in the trenches of HR and understood the unique challenges of that space within the ecosystem of an organization.

And a few additional points for those that are working through your own sense of imposter syndrome when it comes to technology, my own learning journey since 2022, brought some realities into view for me:

1. The tools that used to intimidate me, no longer held that fear. HR would no longer needed to be able to do the complex work of a data analyst to get the insights from the information and data we had available.
2. We shouldn't assume that just because someone does have a technical background, that they are the ideal person or function to oversee the complex space of adopting new tools.

That shift in perspective changed everything for me, because once I started seeing AI as a leadership tool, the real opportunities came into focus. And AI is one of those innovations. It opens up two powerful pathways to success: Productivity and Insights.

On the productivity side, it helps us get more done in less time, without sacrificing quality. It streamlines repetitive tasks, reduces decision fatigue, and frees us up to focus on the work that actually requires human judgment and creativity.

On the insights side, it finally gives us the ability to make sense of the mountain of meaningful data we've been sitting on for years. Data we've lacked the time, tools, or skills to interpret... until now. AI doesn't just organize it; it activates it, helping us make smarter, faster, more strategic decisions. Together, these pathways don't just make work easier. They make it smarter, more human-centered, and more aligned with the future of HR.

A Note on AI Tools

The AI landscape is evolving fast. New tools, features, and capabilities are emerging constantly, and what works well today may soon be replaced by something better. Instead of trying to capture every tool in this book, I share regular updates and curated recommendations on my website, peoplepower.ai.

There, you'll find the latest insights on which AI solutions are actually delivering value in HR, along with use cases, resources, and reflections on a range of AI for HR topics. I encourage you to check in regularly or consider requesting access to my people-power.ai community, and stay curious. Because staying informed is critical for leading strategically.

2.1 Reinventing Recruitment: AI as Your Talent Acquisition Sidekick

Picture this: It's Monday morning. You're checking your inbox for responses to the new role you published on Friday afternoon and expecting a good influx of resumes over the weekend. And the weekend delivered... you've got over a thousand applications waiting for you to review. Sound familiar?

This is the reality for so many recruitment teams leading talent acquisition and the influx is amplified through the waves of layoffs that have been announced across industries, as well as the candidate tools available for mass distribution of resumes. Sifting through hundreds of resumes, trying to spot the gems can feel like searching for a needle in a haystack, except the haystack keeps growing.

Recruiting has always been a balancing act: speed versus quality, volume versus precision. One moment, you're excited to find the perfect hire, and the next, you're buried under a mountain of resumes, each one demanding attention. I remember the grind all too well from my College Recruiting days at News Corp, where reviewing thousands of applications felt like an endurance test.

Back then, we relied on long hours and manual effort. Today, the influx of information is the same, but our approach to selection has changed.

This is where GenAI can provide much needed support for overburdened TA teams serving as a super-powered Recruitment Coordinator. One that sorts, analyzes, and prioritizes candidates in minutes, freeing you up to focus on what really matters, building connections and making great hires.

Let's explore how AI is redefining talent acquisition and making recruitment smarter, not harder.

Crafting Compelling Job Postings

Remember the days of recycling old job descriptions or spending hours wordsmithing every bullet point? GenAI can now help you go far beyond formatting or editing in that it can help you design smarter job posting strategies that attract more aligned, more diverse candidates with less manual work.

Yes, many of you may be using GenAI tools to rewrite job descriptions, but the real opportunity is in how AI can help you craft, test, and optimize the entire job posting strategy. Here's what that can look like:

- Generate role descriptions that align with your company's voice, values, and DEI goals, not just titles and tasks.
- Consider analyzing the key behaviors that best align with a role and include that in your prompts
- Run A/B tests on job title variations and language tone to predict which postings will attract a broader, more qualified candidate pool
- Prompt your AI to analyze past hiring data to recommend job board placements based on success rates by role type or geography
- Use AI to tailor postings by candidate audience such as entry-level, executive, remote, tech-forward, etc., and create messaging that resonates at the specific level you are targeting
- Create tailored outreach messages or social snippets for different platforms (LinkedIn, Slack communities, newsletters, etc.) to extend your job post reach. What about targeting messaging for employee referrals?
- Continuously feed back hiring outcomes and candidate feedback to refine your prompts and improve results over time

This isn't about using these tools for simple editing, it's about leveling up your talent attraction strategy all together. Thinking at the process level, not task level. And it makes a difference! One company I worked with saw a 30% increase in diverse applicants simply by using AI to test and refine the tone, structure, and placement of their job postings.

Equity Check:
Language Shapes Access

Job descriptions are often the first, and sometimes the only, thing a candidate sees. The language we use in them sends clear messages about who belongs, who is qualified, and who should apply. Even subtle word choices can influence who opts in and who self-selects out. With AI, we have the opportunity not just to move faster, but to move more intentionally.

One way to uncover hidden bias in job descriptions is to intentionally prompt your AI tools to flag or rewrite language that might unintentionally signal exclusion.

If you're looking to make your prompts more equity-aware, here are a few examples to guide how you frame them:

- "Review this job description for any language that may discourage applicants from underrepresented backgrounds. Suggest more inclusive alternatives."
- "Rewrite this posting to reduce corporate jargon and make it more accessible to applicants from nontraditional career paths."
- "Check this job description for gendered language and rephrase using neutral, inclusive terms."
- "Adjust this copy to ensure it's appealing to candidates with disabilities, caregivers returning to the workforce, and those without four-year degrees."
- "Generate a version of this job post that reflects our commitment to equity and psychological safety."

Prompting in this way doesn't just clean up language. It becomes a meaningful tool to reduce bias at the top of your hiring funnel and sends a signal to every potential applicant about what kind of workplace they're stepping into.

Resume Screening on Steroids

GenAI takes resume screening to a whole new level. It doesn't just look for keywords; it understands context and can even infer skills that aren't explicitly stated. For example:

- Prompt your AI tool to look for transferable skills across functions or industries based on core capabilities, not just past job titles
- Use AI to analyze which resume attributes have historically predicted success in your company, then prioritize those patterns in future screenings
- Pair AI screening with blind review techniques to reduce unconscious bias during the first resume review phase
- Generate candidate summaries for hiring managers that highlight *why* a candidate is a fit, especially when that fit isn't obvious on paper
- Feed feedback from interviewers or hiring managers back into the AI tool to improve how it scores or surfaces resumes in the future
- Test and refine prompt strategies to differentiate between "qualified" and "well-aligned" candidates, depending on the hiring goal

When used strategically, AI can surface candidates who might otherwise be overlooked... people with high potential, transferable skills, and valuable experience that doesn't follow a conventional path.

AI can also help you identify patterns that predict success, not just based on current fit, but long-term potential. By analyzing performance data from previous hires, AI tools can surface which resume signals are associated with ramp speed, retention, or leadership growth. Used wisely, this kind of insight helps refine your criteria and move from reactive screening to proactive talent strategy.

Imagine a hiring team rethinking their assumptions after the AI highlights a candidate whose background doesn't match the usual checklist. Maybe they've transitioned industries, built skills in nontraditional settings, or taken an unconventional career route. On paper, it might look like a mismatch. But in practice, that candidate brings fresh insight, adaptability, and untapped potential.

Moments like these do more than improve a single hire. They begin to shift how hiring managers define readiness, evaluate value, and expand their understanding of what a successful candidate looks like. That's not just a win for talent strategy, it's a win for equity, innovation, and long-term performance.

Equity Check:
Watch for Hidden Bias

While AI can streamline resume screening, it can also replicate historical inequities. If your hiring data has favored certain schools, titles, or formats, the system may unconsciously reinforce those patterns, unintentionally disadvantaging candidates from underrepresented backgrounds or those with nontraditional experience. This includes people with disabilities, neurodiverse talent, and those with employment gaps or alternative career paths. As HR leaders, we must pair AI tools with inclusive design, ethical training data, and constant monitoring to ensure opportunity is expanded... not narrowed.

Consider including this language in your prompts:

- "Analyze this candidate pool for patterns that may reflect bias in past hiring decisions."
- "Flag resume matches that meet criteria but deviate from historical norms to increase diversity in screening."
- "Review top candidates and suggest additional profiles that demonstrate similar potential but from different backgrounds."

Personalized Candidate Communication
This is where GenAI really shines. It can craft personalized, intentional communication throughout the candidate journey from emails, follow-up messaging, and responding to candidate questions.

Here are some ideas to maximize personalization:

- Generate welcome messages that reflect the candidate's role, location, and hiring manager's tone, not just the standard "We're excited to have you" template
- Create tailored onboarding communications that align with your company's voice and reinforce cultural norms, key values, or team traditions
- Use AI to develop customized FAQs or resource guides based on department, level, or first-day tasks so that new hires feel seen and supported
- Draft pre-start email sequences that build excitement, answer common questions, and create a sense of connection before day one
- Support managers in writing personalized outreach or day-one notes by prompting AI to include specific team references, shared goals, or project context

At one of my fractional clients, we implemented a more curated and personalized communication approach for new hires, using AI to help managers tailor onboarding messages for early touchpoints. It wasn't flashy, but it made a difference. Several new hires called it out directly, saying it felt like the company had taken the time to make their experience personal. That kind of attention in the earliest days matters. As we all know, the relationship building for retention with a new hire starts it starts in those early days and is maximized the moment they feel seen.

AI Assistants: Your 24/7 Candidate Concierge
The reality is that candidates aren't always looking for roles or ready to ask questions during the traditional 9-to-5 window.

With AI Assistants, we can create access when candidates seek the information they need by answering questions, scheduling interviews, and even conducting initial screenings.

But this isn't chatbots as glorified FAQ systems or the "Clippy" of the past (extra points if you had to look up Clippy).

The interactions are so much better as AI Assistants use natural language processing to engage in conversations that feel natural and personal, not scripted.

Used intentionally, they can do far more than reduce recruiter workloads, they can improve the entire candidate experience. Imagine an assistant that not only answers "What's the dress code?" but also shares a link to your culture page, names the hiring manager they'll be meeting, and includes tips from successful candidates who've already gone through the process.

Here's how AI Assistants can level up your candidate journey:

- Provide 24/7 responses that go beyond logistics and actually reinforce your employer brand and culture
- Help candidates feel more prepared by proactively offering interview tips, timelines, and tailored onboarding prep
- Surface candidate concerns earlier by analyzing patterns in questions and sentiment across interactions

- Free up recruiter time by handling repetitive tasks, while still escalating nuanced conversations to a human

Done well, these tools aren't just time-savers, they're relationship builders. And for candidates who are used to ghosting or boilerplate replies, that kind of thoughtful interaction sets a different tone from day one.

And you don't need to build a chatbot from scratch to use AI as a relationship-builder. Whether you start with a custom GPT/Assistant to prototype the experience, partner with a conversational AI platform that specializes in candidate experience, or tap into features inside your current ATS, the key is to treat the assistant like a *personality*, not a script. Make it helpful, real, and reflective of your culture, and it can become a surprisingly effective extension of your team.

Exercise:
Rethinking Your Process
Let's pause here and try something out. Think about your current recruitment process. Where do you spend most of your time? Is it screening resumes? Answering candidate queries? Trying to predict who will be a good fit?

Jot down your top three time consuming recruitment tasks or pain points.

Now, reflecting on what we've covered. How might AI help

with each of these? Don't worry about the specifics of implementation just yet. For now, let your imagination run wild with the possibilities.

Interview Question Generation

Interview preparation takes time, and inconsistency between interviewers often weakens the candidate experience. GenAI can support this process by helping teams generate sharper, more aligned question sets that reflect both the role and your organization's values.

Here's how to get more strategic with this:

- Generate tailored interview guides based on a candidate's resume and the job description, even pre-interview assessment results with suggested areas to focus on based on the job requirements
- Request behavioral or situational questions tied to your core values, cultural traits, or team dynamics
- Ask the AI to generate follow-up questions that probe deeper based on a candidate's background, experience gaps, or areas of curiosity
- Use the same prompt structure across interviewers to create a consistent candidate experience and reduce random variability in how people are evaluated

Done in these ways, AI doesn't just save time, it improves the quality and consistency of your interviews. When every candidate is evaluated with thoughtful, values-aligned questions, you reduce randomness and increase fairness across the board.

You also give hiring managers better tools for deeper conversations. And more meaningful insights from interviewers, making it easier to spot candidates who really stand out, getting you closer to the right hire, faster.

Ethics Check:
Interview Questions Aren't Neutral by Default
When using AI to generate interview questions, it's easy to assume the results are neutral, but that's rarely the case. If your AI tool is trained on biased data or generic question banks, it may suggest questions that disadvantage certain candidates or reinforce narrow definitions of "fit." Watch out for:

- Over reliance on credential-based or institutional-centric questions
- Value judgments embedded in tone (e.g., "Tell me why you failed" vs. "What did you learn from a challenge?")
- Lack of cultural or neurodiversity sensitivity in communication-style questions
- Questions that skew toward extroversion, assertiveness, or Western norms

Always review and refine AI-generated questions through the lens of inclusion. Better yet, involve diverse reviewers in evaluating the content before it's used in live interviews.

Candidate Sentiment Analysis

For a long period of my career, initial interviews were always done by phone. Now I can't imagine not using video throughout the interview process. That being said, video and meeting tools now come with built-in transcription and analysis features, often including sentiment detection. These tool embed natural language processing, and visual can identify changes in tone, flag emotional language, and suggest whether a candidate sounds confident, uncertain, enthusiastic, or disengaged.

It's easy to see how this can support interviewers, especially in high-volume or early-career hiring. But it also introduces new dynamics: candidates may not know their tone is being interpreted, and HR teams may not realize how or where sentiment data is being generated or stored.

There's also something else to consider. As transcription and AI assistant tools become more common, candidates themselves are using them. You may have seen transcribers recording interviews, perhaps to assist candidates in reflecting on what they said, how they said it, and how they felt. The interview is no longer just your moment to evaluate... it's becoming a two-way learning opportunity, powered by tools on both sides.

As sentiment analysis becomes more embedded into standard platforms, HR leaders need to be intentional about how it's used, and how it's communicated. Here are some questions to ask when evaluating sentiment tools in interviews:

- What tools in our current tech stack are already capturing sentiment, even if we're not actively using that feature?
- Are we informing candidates that transcription or sentiment tracking is part of the process, and is that disclosure legally required in our region?
- What are we doing with the data once it's captured? Is it being used, stored, or simply existing in the background?
- Are we training hiring teams to use sentiment insights as conversation starters and not conclusions?
- Are we prepared for candidates to use their own transcription and analysis tools and how does that change our approach?

These questions aren't just operational. They're cultural. How we use sentiment data says a lot about how we view people, trust, and transparency.

Ethics Check:
Sentiment Is a Two-Way Mirror
The tools may offer powerful insights, but it's our job to ensure those insights are used responsibly. Before sentiment analysis becomes part of your hiring process, or continues to operate unnoticed in the background, it's worth pausing to ask what it reflects about your values. That's where ethics enters the conversation.

AI can now capture how candidates show up in interviews. But it can also reflect how your organization shows up. How clearly it communicates, how fairly it evaluates, and how transparently it discloses what's being tracked.

Before relying on sentiment insights:

- Make sure your process is compliant with recording and data-use laws in every hiring jurisdiction
- Communicate clearly and early about what tools are in use and why
- Treat tone as one piece of context, not as evidence
- Assume candidates are analyzing your side of the conversation, too

The tools are here. The question is how we choose to use them.

Final Thought

Recruitment is no longer just a function of speed or scale. It's a reflection of how your organization shows up to the world. With AI, you have the tools to build a hiring experience that is more inclusive, more intentional, and more aligned with the values you want your future employees to see. The opportunity isn't just to fill roles faster. It's to design a process that respects the time and unique potential of everyone who enters it. That's the kind of recruitment that retains. That's the kind of recruitment that earns trust.

2.2 Reimagining Learning and Development

When I first started in Learning and Development back in 1998, our biggest technological leap was moving from overhead projectors to PowerPoint. Now, as I look at the L&D landscape, I feel a mix of excitement and awe at the potential of AI to transform how we approach workplace learning. It's not just another tool in our kit; it's a mental shift that will redefine how we develop talent in our organizations.

Content backlogs. Outdated materials. Feedback you'll get to when you can find the time. If you've spent any time in L&D, you know the rhythm, and the constant tension between what you *want* to build and what you *have* the capacity to deliver. AI is already starting to change the equation.

Instead of scrambling to keep up, you now have a partner that can help you build faster, personalize smarter, and make space for the kind of learning experiences you actually want to create. Not cookie-cutter compliance courses. Not endless slide decks. Real, targeted development that feels timely, relevant, and human. AI isn't here to replace the judgment, intuition, and design instincts that make L&D impactful. It's here to give those things room to breathe.

The Promise of True Personalization
We've been talking about the potential of personalized learning for years haven't we? It's been the holy grail of L&D, always just

out of reach due to the sheer complexity of tailoring content to individual needs at scale.

Picture an AI system that can analyze an employee's performance data, career aspirations, and learning style, then craft a learning journey that adapts in real time to their progress. It's not about cold, impersonal algorithms making decisions. It's about giving us the tools to offer every employee the kind of personalized attention we'd love to provide if we had unlimited time and resources.

But here's where we need to be thoughtful. As we implement AI driven personalization tools, we need to consider:

- Data privacy and ethical use of employee information
- Ensuring AI recommendations don't reinforce existing biases or limit opportunities
- Maintaining a balance between AI guided learning paths and employee agency in their development

Reflection Point

How could AI driven personalization address current gaps in your L&D offerings? What ethical considerations would you need to address in your organization?

Content Creation: Your New Creative Partner

Let's talk about one of the most time consuming aspects of our work: content creation. How many hours have you spent staring at a blank page trying to come up with the perfect scenario for leadership training? Or sifting through mountains of resources to curate the right content for a new onboarding program?

We have an opportunity to look at creation through a different lens, because GenAI is like having a tireless creative partner, always ready with a fresh idea or a new perspective. In the new creation process, you might find yourself outlining the key points you want to cover in a training session, and let AI generate a first draft of the content, complete with relevant examples and interactive elements.

But that's just the beginning. Here are some ways L&D teams can activate AI to accelerate and elevate content creation:

- Draft eLearning modules, onboarding guides, or internal playbooks based on role-specific goals, policies, or behavioral expectations
- Repackage existing content, like leadership frameworks, DEI commitments, or performance tools into bite-sized formats for mobile, video, or blended learning
- Generate quizzes, reflection prompts, or discussion questions that reinforce key concepts and encourage deeper learner engagement
- Translate high-level strategies into role-based scenarios that feel practical, realistic, and directly tied to the learner's day-to-day experience

- Localize content or rewrite materials for different audiences (entry-level vs. exec-level, field teams vs. HQ, etc.) with tone and context sensitivity
- Turn learner feedback into content improvements by prompting AI to summarize open-ended responses and suggest refinements

In this model, AI is a collaborator that helps you move faster from insight to impact, freeing up your time for what matters most: designing learning experiences that lead to real behavior change.

As you experiment with AI in content creation, keep these points in mind:

- Always review and refine AI generated content to ensure it aligns with your organization's voice and values
- Use AI as a brainstorming tool to overcome creative blocks and generate diverse ideas
- Leverage AI to keep your content up-to-date with the latest industry trends and best practices

Exercise:
Building Learning with AI
Take a common training area, such as your company onboarding, performance management, or leadership development, and experiment with using an AI tool to generate a outline or initial draft focused on a target function.

1. What part of the process felt faster, easier, or more efficient with AI involved?

2. Where did the content feel off, flat, or lacking context where you need to add your human touch?

3. How might this change the way you approach content creation in the future?

Breaking Down Global Barriers

In our increasingly globalized workplaces, making learning content relevant across diverse cultures and languages has become increasingly more challenging. I remember working on a global leadership program and the headache of trying to make it culturally relevant across 3 different countries... it was difficult and I spent more time than I like to admit course correcting for elements that weren't relevant from one geography to the next.

GenAI offers exciting possibilities in this area including systems that don't just translate your content but adapt it culturally, suggesting appropriate local examples or adjusting scenarios to fit different cultural contexts. Now, let me be clear, it shouldn't replace human cultural insight, but it can give us a more nuanced starting point that's much closer to the mark.

As you explore AI for localization and cultural adaptation, consider:

- The importance of human review to ensure cultural nuances are accurately captured
- Using AI to identify potentially sensitive content that might need special attention in different cultural contexts
- Leveraging AI to create more inclusive content that resonates with diverse audiences

Reflection Point

Think about a recent training program you've developed. How could AI assisted localization have made it more accessible and relevant to a global audience? What challenges might you anticipate in implementing such a system?

Adaptive Learning and Assessment

We've all been in those training sessions where half the room is bored because the content is too basic, while the other half is lost because it's over their heads. Adaptive learning leveraging AI could make those scenarios obsolete.

Envision a learning module that adjusts its difficulty and content in real time based on each learner's responses. It goes beyond branching... it would be like having a personal tutor for every employee, ensuring they're always in that sweet spot of challenge and engagement. And when it comes to assessment, we can move beyond multiple-choice quizzes to adaptive scenarios that test not just knowledge, but the application of skills in realistic situations.

Begin activating adaptive learning and assessment with AI:

To bring this to life, we need to move beyond static content and start thinking like designers of responsive, personalized learning ecosystems. AI makes it possible to adjust not just what we teach, but curate the how and when, based on signals from each learner. Some ideas for moving in this direction include:

- Use AI tools to break down existing courses into modular content chunks categorized by difficulty, topic, or skill level
- Prompt AI to recommend learning paths based on prior role history, performance data, or pre-assessment results
- Develop short-form microlearning moments that can be swapped in or out dynamically based on learner engagement or pacing
- Analyze completion and performance data to identify where learning paths lose traction and adapt content accordingly
- Create messaging that explains to learners how and why their experience is changing, reinforcing trust in the personalization process

As you consider implementing adaptive learning and assessment, keep in mind:

- The need for a robust content library to support truly adaptive learning paths
- The importance of transparent communication to learners; how and why their learning experience is adapting
- Using the rich data from adaptive assessments to inform broader L&D strategies and identify organizational skill gaps

Reflection Point

How could adaptive learning address current challenges in your training programs? What skills or topics in your organization would benefit most from this approach?

The Human AI Partnership in L&D

As exciting as all this sounds, it's crucial to remember that AI is a tool, not a magic wand. The real power of AI in L&D will come from how we, as L&D professionals, learn to work alongside it. It's about finding the right balance between AI driven efficiency and human led strategy and connection.

As we step forward to understand the changes AI will bring in L&D, we have the opportunity to reshape how people learn and grow in the workplace. But with that opportunity comes the responsibility to implement these tools ethically, to ensure they're enhancing, rather than replacing, human connection.

And our real role will be to guide our organizations through this transformation.

Here are some key considerations as you navigate through your teams' learning journey:

- Develop your AI literacy to make informed decisions about AI implementation in your L&D programs
- Stay focused on learning outcomes and learner experience, using AI as a means to enhance these, not as an end in itself
- Be prepared to evolve your L&D roles, focusing more on strategy, ethical considerations, and the uniquely human aspects of learning

Final Thought

As you consider your own L&D challenges and aspirations, where do you see AI making the biggest impact? How might it change your role, and what new skills do you think you'll need to develop to thrive in this AI augmented future of L&D?

Remember, we're not just passive observers as AI becomes more a part of the way we work. We're have the opportunity to shape how these tools are used in our organizations. So let's approach this new chapter with curiosity, critical thinking, and a commitment to leveraging AI to create more impactful, accessible, and personalized learning experiences for all.

In our next section, we'll explore how GenAI is set to transform another critical area of HR: Performance Management. But before we move on, take a moment to reflect on how these AI driven changes in L&D might cascade out to affect other aspects of employee development and organizational culture.

2.3 Performance Management Reimagined

THE OPINIONS on the need for Performance Reviews are as wide as the ocean. I've spent years reviewing hundreds of annual reviews in excel spreadsheets to navigating new technology for more frequent, tech enabled platforms. Those nerve wracking sessions where a year's worth of work was condensed into a single conversation, often leaving both managers and employees feeling the mission was left unmet. Well hold on, because AI has the potential to turn performance management on its head.

Continuous Feedback: The New Normal
In our new paradigm, feedback isn't just given in scheduled meetings but is a constant, organic part of the work process. AI is making this a reality.

But the transformation doesn't stop with employees. For managers, this shift is just as profound. No longer are they burdened with evaluating performance based on fleeting observations or incomplete recollections. Instead of relying on what they happened to see in the moment, or what stands out most in their memory, they now have access to a rich and continuous compilation of data.

AI tools can now provide real time dashboards that capture key contributions, track patterns of growth, and identify opportunities for coaching. AI can support managers to recognize trends, not just moments. Highlighting the big wins that might otherwise go unnoticed, as well as areas where additional support is needed, and even suggests when an employee might be ready for more responsibility.

With AI acting as a powerful assistant, managers can move beyond the stress of performance evaluations based on fragmented information, and instead focus on having deeper, more meaningful conversations. They can offer feedback that is more precise, contextual, and actionable, creating a workplace where development isn't an annual event but an ongoing process of growth and recognition.

Ways to leverage AI for continuous feedback:

- Use AI-enabled pulse surveys to capture real-time employee sentiment and surface trends across teams or time periods
- Analyze feedback data to identify recurring themes and patterns, helping managers focus their conversations on what matters most

- Prompt AI tools to summarize feedback from multiple sources: self-assessments, peer reviews, customer input, into a single narrative to support 1:1s
- Experiment with AI-generated coaching prompts that suggest how a manager might frame feedback in different scenarios
- Deploy intelligent nudges that recommend timely feedback moments based on task completion, milestones, or behavioral patterns
- Track and visualize skill development over time, giving employees a clearer view of progress and areas for growth

And for teams still relying on manual processes, start by exploring AI tools that integrate with the platforms you already use. Look for systems that can layer onto your existing HRIS, performance, or communication tools, rather than those requiring a full tech overhaul. Then evaluate not just the software cost, but the time cost of manual feedback cycles, the inconsistency of data, and the missed opportunity for strategic insight. The question isn't whether AI is more efficient, it's whether your current approach is still worth the effort.

However, we need to be considerate and tread carefully:

Visualize this scenario: You're working on a project and as you complete each task, an AI assistant reviews your work, comparing it to best practices and past successful projects. It offers real-time suggestions for improvement, celebrates your wins, and even predict

- How do we ensure that this constant feedback doesn't become overwhelming or demotivating?
- How do we maintain the human touch in performance management when AI is providing so much of the day-to-day feedback?

Reflection Point
How could continuous, AI driven feedback change the dynamic between managers and employees in your organization? What challenges and opportunities do you foresee?

Predictive Performance Analysis
One of the most exciting aspects of AI in performance management: its predictive capabilities. Imagine being able to identify potential performance issues before they become problems, or spotting high-potential employees early in their careers.

GenAI can analyze patterns in employee behavior, work output, and even communication styles to predict future performance. It's like having a crystal ball but one based on data and machine learning rather than magic. And these insights don't just shape how we review performance, they can also shape how we grow it.

For example, the AI might notice that an employee's communication with their team has become less frequent and their project completions are slowing down. It could flag this to the manager as a potential sign of disengagement or burnout, allowing for early intervention.

As we implement these predictive tools, we need to consider:

- The ethical implications of using AI to make predictions about employee performance
- How to communicate these predictions to employees in a way that's constructive, not anxiety inducing
- The importance of using AI predictions as one input among many, not as the sole basis for decisions about an employee's future

Reflection Point

If you had a reliable way to predict employee performance, how would it change your approach to talent development and succession planning? What safeguards would you put in place to ensure fair and ethical use of this technology?

Personalized Development Plans

One size fits all? Not anymore. GenAI is enabling us to create hyper-personalized development plans for each employee.

By analyzing an employee's performance data, career aspirations, and learning style, AI can generate tailored development plans that adapt in real time based on the employee's progress and changing organizational needs.

One of the 'magic' elements of AI is its ability to identify core characteristics for individual employees and suggest specific training, stretch assignments, or mentorship opportunities based on an employee's unique development needs. It's like having a personal career coach for every employee in your organization.

But let's not forget the human element. As we implement these AI driven development plans, we need to consider:

- How to balance AI recommendations with employee agency and manager insights
- The importance of regular human check-ins to ensure the AI generated plan aligns with the employee's evolving goals and the organization's needs
- How to use AI generated plans as a starting point for meaningful career development conversations, not as a replacement for them

Exercise:
Supporting Development with AI

Choose an employee you're currently supporting, or select a sample role you frequently develop within your organization. Then, use an AI tool to generate a personalized development plan based on that role's skills, growth potential, and goals. You can feed it content such as:

- A job description or role profile
- A summary of recent performance feedback

- A list of skills or development areas tied to career progression
- High-level goals the employee has shared (or that the role demands)

Prompt the AI to build a draft development plan, including ideas for learning content, stretch assignments, mentorship opportunities, or short-term projects.

Then, reflect:

1. What parts of the plan felt accurate, helpful, or immediately usable and how might they enhance the speed or quality of development conversations?
2. Where did the AI-generated content fall short or lack personalization, and what required your judgment, cultural context, or manager input?
3. How could AI change the way you design development plans in the future? Could it support more frequent check-ins, broader access to growth pathways, or more scalable manager support?

Goal Setting and Measures

Setting objectives and key results (OKRs), KPI's, SmartGoals, or any other structured goal measurement process is crucial for aligning individual performance with organizational goals. But let's be honest, it can be a challenging and time consuming process.

Not only the decision making process at the executive level, but once those decisions are made, so much time and effort is required to create meaningful cascades of those goals, and tying them to the motivation and purpose at the individual contributor level is important... but also a huge time commitment.

Goal setting itself isn't new, but our approach to it can be. AI allows us to move beyond static, top-down processes and build something more adaptive, collaborative, and scalable. It's not just about writing goals faster. It's about building a system that makes goals meaningful at every level. With the right prompts and inputs, AI can support your team in the the goal-setting process, from strategic alignment to individual clarity. Here's how to start exploring what that looks like in practice:

- Provide prompt examples to help managers phrase individual goals in clearer, more actionable, and measurable language, especially when rolling goals down to front-line teams
- Feed AI your organization's mission, values, and performance framework to generate goals that are aligned not just to metrics, but to culture
- Analyze progress updates and performance data to surface when individuals or teams are veering off track and suggest corrective action
- Identify interdependencies across OKRs that may be missed, where team or department objectives are working in silos or at cross-purposes

- Use AI-generated summaries of goal progress to fuel more frequent, focused 1:1 conversations and team check-ins

Reflection Point

What would it look like to shift from goal setting as a quarterly event to a continuous conversation? Where could AI help your teams stay aligned, and where will the human touch still matter most?

The Future of Performance Reviews

Now I'm not saying AI will completely replace traditional performance reviews (though some of my best friends are in that camp), but it will certainly transform them. With AI providing continuous feedback and predictive insights, performance reviews can become forward looking strategy sessions rather than backward looking evaluations.

In a perfect future, there will be a time when walking into a performance review is viewed as a win-win conversation. Where employees and managers have access to a comprehensive, AI generated report of performance over the past period. This report doesn't just cover what was achieved; it highlights deep insights into your work patterns, collaboration style, and areas of potential growth.

The conversation can then evolve to focus on interpreting this data, setting future goals, and strategizing on how to leverage your strengths as well as address your development areas. It's a much more productive and less stressful experience for everyone involved.

As we move towards this AI enhanced review process, consider:

- How to train managers to effectively use AI generated insights in their reviews
- The importance of maintaining a human-centric approach using AI data to inform, not dictate, the conversation
- How to ensure employees feel empowered, not surveilled, by this data rich approach to performance management

Final Thought

The transformation of performance management through AI will reshape how managers approach their work in the coming years. What new skills will managers need to develop to thrive in this new environment?

Remember, the goal of all this AI powered performance management isn't to remove the human element. It's to enhance it. By leveraging AI to handle data analysis and provide ongoing feedback, we free up time and mental space for what really matters: having meaningful conversations, building relationships, and helping our employees grow and succeed.

In our next section we'll explore how GenAI is set to transform Employee Experience and Engagement. As you'll see, the ripple effects of AI in performance management will have a significant impact on how employees experience and engage with their work and their organization.

2.4 Elevating Employee Experience and Engagement

When I first started in HR, "employee experience" wasn't even a term we used. We talked about job satisfaction and employee morale but the idea of crafting a holistic experience throughout the employee lifecycle? That came later. And now, with GenAI entering the picture, we're on the cusp of a revolution in how we approach employee experience and engagement.

Let's dive into this brave new world and explore how AI is set to transform the way employees interact with their work, their colleagues, and their organization.

Personalized Employee Journeys
Remember when personalization in the workplace meant remembering your colleagues' birthday? GenAI can take personalization to a whole new level.
AI systems can craft a unique employee journey for each individual in your organization, from the moment they're hired to their eventual departure (or retirement, if you're doing things right!). This AI doesn't just look at job titles and departments –

it considers an employee's skills, career aspirations, learning style, and communication preferences.

For example, a new hire might receive a personalized onboarding plan that not only covers the essentials of their role but also connects them with mentors who match their career interests, suggests employee resource groups based on their background and interests, and even recommends lunch spots near the office that align with their dietary preferences.

As exciting as this sounds, we need to consider:

- How to balance personalization with a sense of shared organizational culture
- The ethical implications of using personal data to craft these experiences
- Ensuring that AI driven personalization doesn't inadvertently create silos or echo chambers within the organization

Reflection Point
How could hyper-personalized employee journeys change the way people experience work in your organization? What opportunities and challenges do you foresee?

AI Powered Internal Communications
Let's talk about the eternal challenge of internal communications. How many times have you sent out an important company-wide email only to realize later that half the employees

didn't even open it? Part of the reality of mass communication is attempting to reach everyone with the same message and breaking through the other messages they have.

That's where AI can help. Not by replacing communication, but by making it smarter, more targeted, and more responsive to how people actually engage.

Systems that can:

- Craft personalized communication for each employee taking into account their role, interests, and communication style
- Determine the optimal time and channel to deliver each message for maximum engagement
- Analyze the effectiveness of communications and continuously improve its approach

It's not just about top-down communication. AI can build better peer-to-peer and bottom-up communication too. Think of AI powered collaboration tools that can suggest the right colleagues to involve in a project, or sentiment analysis tools that can gauge employee mood and flag potential issues before they become problems. Here are a few ways to start exploring how AI can support and scale internal communications, without losing the human tone or purpose behind them:

- Use generative AI tools to rewrite internal messages in

different tones or reading levels depending on audience, field teams, managers, execs, etc.

- Prompt AI to summarize long or technical updates into short, clear versions for different channels like email, Slack, or intranet posts
- Experiment with A/B versions of headlines, subject lines, and calls to action to see what increases open and engagement rates
- Track patterns in message engagement (opens, clicks, replies) to identify the best time of day, format, or channel for your audience
- Use AI to translate messages across languages or rewrite content for cultural clarity in global or distributed teams
- Analyze feedback or sentiment from responses to internal comms to help shape future messaging strategy

As we implement these AI communication tools we need to consider the importance of maintaining authenticity in communications even when AI is involved in crafting the message and how to ensure important broad information doesn't get lost in the sea of personalized communication.

Exercise:
AI to the comms rescue
Think about a recent company-wide communication... an email, newsletter, policy rollout, or announcement. Use an AI tool to revisit and improve it. You might:

- Rewrite the message with different tones or reading levels to fit various employee audiences
- Summarize the content into shorter formats for Slack, intranet, or mobile delivery
- Generate alternative subject lines or headers for better visibility and engagement
- Ask AI to analyze clarity, length, and sentiment, and suggest improvements

Then, reflect:

1. What changed when you involved AI in the communication process: tone, clarity, format, or reach?

2. How would you measure the success of AI-enhanced communication in your org (e.g., engagement rates, comprehension, feedback)?

3. Where do you still need human context, oversight, or tone-setting to make your message land?

Engagement Prediction and Proactive Intervention

We've always cared about how employees feel at work, but we've rarely had the tools to design that experience with real intentionality. Employee engagement surveys have been a staple of HR for years, and if we are honest, they have fallen short. Too time consuming with little to no real actions taken from the feedback. Employees poo poo the process because the results haven't met the promises.

And if you've heard me talk about surveys, you'll know that the old staple of relying on Likert scale questions with one or two comment questions at the end, isn't going to bring our business the meaty insights that influence change. Insights we need to reverse the challenge of disconnection that employees are feeling right now.

NLP and GenAI makes this possible. By analyzing a wide range of data points, from survey data and email sentiment to project participation rates, and even the tone of voice in recorded meetings, AI can provide a continuous pulse on employee engagement.

Exercise:
Rethinking How You Measure Engagement

Choose a recent engagement survey, or skip it and just consider the last time you were asked to assess "how your people are doing." Then, walk through these steps:

1. Identify your current data sources. Where does employee feedback come from today? Surveys? Exit interviews? 1:1s? Team meetings? Is it structured or anecdotal?

2. Audit the lag. How long does it take to collect, analyze, and act on that data? How much gets lost in interpretation? What's being filtered through bias or political pressure?

3. Consider how AI might change your view. What signals are you not capturing? Tone in emails, project participation, real-

time feedback trends? What could a live dashboard of engagement data *do* for your CEO, your Board, or your managers?

Take a moment to reflect on :

- What would you gain by seeing patterns earlier?
- What would your teams gain by being heard in real time?
- Where would you still need humans to step in, with care, context, and conversation?

Beyond Reflection to Prediction

More importantly, it can predict potential drops in engagement before they happen. Using AI, it's possible to get an alert that a high-performing employee might be at risk of burnout. Or data that indicates a team's engagement is likely to dip due to an upcoming challenging project.

This predictive capability allows for proactive intervention. Instead of reacting to disengagement after it happens, we can take steps to prevent it in the first place.

Asking these questions could lead to significantly deeper conversations with employees and lead to greater engagement and understanding.

- How do we implement this kind of monitoring ethically and transparently?

- How do we balance the benefits of proactive intervention with employees' right to privacy?
- How do we ensure that AI driven engagement predictions don't become self-fulfilling prophecies?

Reflection Point

If you had a reliable way to predict employee engagement in real time, how would it change your approach to employee experience? What proactive measures would you put in place?

This level of visibility doesn't just change the game for HR. It transforms decision-making at every level of leadership.

For CEOs:

What would it mean for your CEO to have a pulse on organizational morale at any given moment, with AI aggregating and analyzing sentiment across teams. Instead of relying on outdated engagement surveys or quarterly reports, you could see in real time how leadership decisions, market shifts, or company-wide initiatives are impacting your employees and departments. If engagement starts dipping after a major strategic shift, you don't have to wait for an exit interview to diagnose the problem, you can intervene immediately, adjusting communication strategies, reallocating resources, or providing targeted support where needed.

For Boards of Directors:

The challenge for most boards is that they're making

high-stakes decisions based on lagging indicators: past financial performance, annual engagement scores, and executive reports. But what if they had a real-time dashboard showcasing workforce sentiment, operational bottlenecks, and leadership effectiveness? AI can surface key trends across the company, helping boards assess whether cultural initiatives are resonating, if leadership transitions are stabilizing teams, or whether certain departments are at risk of turnover before it becomes a crisis. Think about how leveraging the insights from AI could provide valuable ROI wins for the organization, and how you could leverage that for greater strategic visibility with your BOD.

For Investors & Stakeholders:
Employee engagement is often a predictor of business performance. AI-powered workforce insights could become an essential part of investor due diligence, helping them assess company culture, leadership effectiveness, and operational efficiency in ways that financial statements alone can't reveal. If engagement is trending downward in a high-growth company, investors could ask the right questions early, ensuring long-term sustainability rather than reacting when problems manifest in attrition or declining performance.

This is about having the right data at the right time. AI doesn't replace human leadership, but it can be leveraged to enhance it, equipping leaders with real-time intelligence to make better decisions, foster stronger cultures, and drive sustainable growth.

AI Enhanced Employee Support

We've all been there. Helping employees find the right form on the company intranet, responding to repetitive questions, or as an employee ourself, waiting on hold with IT to resolve a simple issue.

These small frustrations can add up to a negative employee experience. But as we move towards a world of AI Agents it's already possible for every employee to have a personal AI assistant to help them navigate the complexities of corporate life.

Now, with AI-powered assistants, it's possible to support employees more efficiently, and more personally, at scale. In fact, there are a range of tools, from free to paid, that can power incredibly sophisticated chatbots and virtual assistants that can:

- Answer FAQs about company policies and procedures
- Guide employees through complex processes like benefits enrollment
- Provide frontline IT support for common issues
- Offer career advice and development suggestions

But knowing what these tools *can* do is only the first step. Here are a few ways to start putting AI to work inside your organization to streamline support and improve the day-to-day employee experience:

- Train an AI assistant on your internal documentation including your Handbook, Values, internal policies, IT guides, and benefits materials, so it can provide real-time answers to employee questions
- Create conversational workflows (e.g., "How do I request parental leave?") that guide employees step by step through complex processes
- Use AI to analyze patterns in support tickets or help desk inquiries to identify FAQs and automate common responses
- Enable role-specific support by tailoring AI knowledge bases to different employee groups (new hires, frontline staff, managers, etc.)
- Use AI to draft knowledge base updates based on policy changes or new programs, so your support content stays current without constant manual rewriting
- Reminder: Regularly audit AI responses for accuracy, tone, and alignment with company policy, and set clear escalation rules for when a human needs to step in

The beauty of these AI assistants is that they're available 24/7, never lose patience, and can be continuously updated with the latest information.

But as we implement these AI support systems we need to consider:

- The importance of having clear escalation paths for issues that require human intervention
- How to ensure the AI assistants are giving accurate and up-to-date information
- The potential impact or need for upskilling on human support roles in the organization

Reflection Point

How could AI powered support systems change the day-to-day experience of employees in your organization? What tasks or queries would you prioritize for AI handling?

Crafting Meaningful Work Experiences

Here's where things get really exciting. GenAI has the potential to help us craft more meaningful work experiences for our employees. By analyzing an employee's skills, interests, and career goals, AI could suggest job crafting opportunities. Make recommendations for ways to tweak their current role to align more closely with their passions and strengths, or identify cross-functional projects that offer valuable growth experiences and even help managers assign tasks in ways that maximize both productivity and employee satisfaction.

For example, imagine an AI system recognizing an employee's passion for sustainability based on their learning choices and engagement with sustainability-related topics on the company's social platform. It could then suggest ways to integrate sustainability initiatives into their role or connect them with the company's green team. How do you imagine an employee that had that kind of personal and professional reinforcement of motivations and purpose would feel about working for your company?

That kind of alignment between personal motivation and organizational opportunity doesn't have to be left to chance. With the right tools and prompts, AI can help surface those opportunities at scale. Here are a few ways to start putting that into practice:

- Use AI to analyze employee learning behavior, past project work, or stated career goals to suggest tailored development opportunities
- Prompt AI to identify cross-functional projects or internal opportunities that align with an employee's interests or skill gaps
- Surface tasks that could be shifted, expanded, or reframed within a current role to better match employee strengths or long-term growth areas
- Help managers design personalized stretch assignments by prompting AI to match business needs with employee aspirations
- Review patterns in job crafting suggestions to ensure equitable access and look for which teams or roles get recommended growth paths most often, and address any gaps

Don't forget to include space for employees to flag interests or motivations directly into systems where AI can incorporate them into suggestions.

As we explore these possibilities, we need to consider:

- How to balance AI suggestions with managerial discretion and organizational needs. What training, discussion, escalation and resolution will need to be discussed and considered?
- The potential for AI to help create more equitable access to growth opportunities and ensure that the tools themselves are evaluated for the biases that may create inequality in decision making.
- How to ensure that AI driven job crafting aligns with overall organizational goals

Exercise:
Personalizing Growth Through AI
Take a few minutes to reflect on how your organization currently supports meaningful work and development for employees. Then, consider the following:

1. Think of one high-potential employee on your team or within your organization. What are their strengths, interests, or long-term career goals?

. . .

2. Where in their current role could small adjustments create more engagement, purpose, or skill-building?

3. How might AI tools help identify those opportunities or scale this kind of personalization across more employees?

Use this reflection to begin thinking about job crafting not just as an informal manager skill, but as a system-enabled strategy to help people do more of what matters, while driving real value for the business.

Final Thought

As we explore the impact of AI on employee experience and engagement, we need to consider and determine the role of HR professionals evolving. What new skills will we need to develop to effectively leverage these AI tools while maintaining the human touch that's so crucial in our field?

Remember, the goal of all this AI powered enhancement isn't to automate the employee experience. It's to make it more human. By leveraging AI to handle routine tasks, provide personalized support, and offer data-driven insights, we free up time and resources to focus on what really matters: building genuine connections, fostering a sense of belonging, and helping our employees find meaning and purpose in their work.

Bringing It All Together

As we wrap up this chapter on AI Applications in HR Functions, take a moment to reflect on how these changes in recruitment, learning and development, performance management, and employee experience all interconnect. The future of HR is integrated, personalized, and AI-enhanced... and it's our job to shape this future in a way that benefits both our organizations and our employees.

This chapter wasn't about theory. It was about action.

You've now seen how AI can transform the employee journey from end to end. The next step is yours. Let's talk about what it takes to actually bring these ideas to life.

In our next chapter, we'll dive into the practicalities of implementing AI in HR.
How do we get from where we are now to this AI enhanced future? What challenges might we face along the way? And how do we ensure we're implementing these powerful tools ethically and responsibly?

Chapter 3

Things Getting Real

How to Bring AI into Your HR World

We've covered how AI can enhance HR functions, and you likely see several opportunities for your own organization. But before diving into implementation let's address a critical point: even the most promising AI initiatives can fail without proper planning and execution. Some of the tougher lessons I've learned throughout my own career are that successful implementations require a strategic, methodical approach.

In this chapter, we're going to roll up our sleeves and get into the nitty-gritty of bringing AI into your HR department. We'll cover everything from assessing if your organization is truly ready for AI, to building a bulletproof business case, selecting the right tools and vendors, and managing the change that comes with this technological shift. So, grab your favorite beverage, get comfortable, and let's dive in!

3.1 Assessing AI Readiness in Your Organization

I'm sure many of you can relate to this scenario: you've just returned back to the office from an HR conference, buzzing with excitement about the latest ideas and ways to leverage AI. You're ready to jump in and make AI a part of the team overnight.

Wait! Before you start signing contracts and scheduling demos, let's take a step back and assess if your organization is truly ready for this AI.

Assessing AI readiness isn't just about having the budget or the desire to implement new technology. It's about having the right foundation in place to ensure AI can truly thrive and deliver value in your organization.

Data Readiness: The Fuel for Your AI Engine

As all of us learn through any type of tech integration (HRIS anyone?) AI is only as good as the data it's fed. Think of data as the fuel for your AI engine. If it's low-quality or inconsistent, your AI initiatives will sputter and stall. Here's what you need to look at:

- Data Quality: Is your HR data clean, consistent, and accurate? Or is it a mix of formats, and full of outdated or conflicting information?
- Data Quantity: For those who want to build vs buy, do you have enough historical data to train AI models effectively? Some AI applications might need years of data to perform well.
- Data Integration: Are your HR systems talking to each other, or are they isolated data silos?
- Data Governance: Do you have clear policies and procedures for data management, including data privacy and security?

In early 2024, I worked with a new client eager to implement a specific AI recruitment tool after hearing me speak about it at a conference. They were excited about the potential of streamlining hiring, reducing time-to-fill, and leveraging the built in AI functionality to surface top talent more efficiently. Before we could dig into the integration process, we quickly ran into a major roadblock. Their data was a mess. Job titles were wildly inconsistent, key candidate and employee data was missing, and their existing systems weren't designed to communicate with each other.

True confession time... I've been there. I've also seen this scenario play out time and time again, especially in organizations that have had other functions oversee some HR information (like finance or office admin), and others that had undergone leadership changes, technology upgrades, or rapid scaling.

Data fragmentation is one of the biggest challenges in leveraging AI effectively, and no matter how powerful the tool, it can only be as good as the data feeding it. Instead of pushing forward with an AI solution that would be built on a shaky foundation, we had to take a step back. Our priority became cleaning up their data infrastructure, standardizing job titles, filling in missing information, and ensuring their systems could integrate properly.

This wasn't the detour they had hoped for, but it was a necessary one. By taking the time to fix their data foundation, they would not only set themselves up for AI driven recruitment success, but also improve overall operational efficiency, reporting accuracy, and strategic decision making.

AI isn't a magic fix, it amplifies what's already there. And in this case, we needed to make sure what was there was solid before letting AI do its work.

Technical Infrastructure: Building Your AI Home

Next, let's talk about your technical setup. You wouldn't build a house without a solid foundation, right? The same goes for AI. Unfortunately what I've seen happen far too often is that HR teams aren't equipped to understand the key questions needed to help our overworked tech teams help us determine the best options for integration. So we don't ask and then wait until the tech backlog clears up.

Here are some of the core questions that I've learned in working with IT teams through integrating tools. You will most certainly want talk to your organizations IT/Data/Tech teams to add to this list, and to better understand the answers to these questions.

- Computing Power: Do you have the necessary hardware to run AI algorithms? Some AI applications can be resource intensive.
- Cloud Capabilities: Are you set up to leverage cloud computing for AI if needed?
- Integration Capabilities: Can your current HR systems easily integrate with new AI tools?
- Security Measures: Do you have robust cybersecurity measures in place to protect the sensitive data that AI will be processing?
- IT Support: Does your IT team have the capacity and expertise to support AI implementations?

Reflection Point

Think about past HRIS implementations. What technical hurdles did you face? How might these apply to an AI implementation?

Skills and Expertise: Assembling Your AI Dream Team

AI implementation isn't just a technical project. It requires a unique blend of skills.

Here's what you need to consider:

- Data Science Expertise: If you plan to build tools, do you have technical employees who understand HR data and can build AI models?
- HR Tech Savviness: Is your HR team comfortable with technology and open to AI driven processes?
- AI Literacy Among Leadership: Do your leaders understand both the potential and limitations of AI?
- Change Management Skills: Do you have people who can guide the organization through the transformation that AI will bring?
- Ethical AI Understanding: Is there awareness about the ethical implications of AI in HR?

Don't panic if you're not ticking all these boxes yet. Few organizations are 100% ready for AI from the get. The key is to identify your gaps so you can address them as part of your AI implementation strategy.

Exercise:
Skills and Gaps
Review the five core skill areas above. Now, assess your team's current capabilities in each one on a scale of 1–5 (1 = minimal capability, 5 = strong and consistent). Then, prioritize them

based on urgency for development (1 = highest priority, 5 = lowest priority). This will help you identify the highest-leverage areas for upskilling and partnership.

		Rating	Priority
1	Data Science Expertise		
2	HR Tech Savvy		
3	AI Literacy Among Leadership		
4	Change Management		
5	Ethical AI Awareness		

Building Your AI Dream Team: The Network That Leads Transformation

Most organizations start their AI journey by forming a project team. But AI isn't just a project, it's a shift in how we work, decide, communicate, and lead. It deserves something more dynamic than a static committee. The companies that are moving AI forward responsibly and successfully aren't doing it through org charts. They're doing it through networks of trust, experimentation, and influence.

Your AI Dream Team isn't about titles. It's about your team members that ask better questions, challenge assumptions, and lead with trust. It's a group of capability-builders who will test, shape, and scale the use of AI inside your organization.

Here are five roles, mindsets really, you need in the room:

The Bridge Builder

This person can translate between functions: tech, people, and operations to help everyone see the shared opportunity. They're credible across levels and bring a calm, grounded presence to ambiguity. Often a seasoned HRBP, a systems-minded ops partner, or someone who's earned trust by consistently connecting the dots.

The Challenger

You need someone who will slow things down when it feels too shiny, too fast, or too shallow. They'll raise ethical flags, pressure-test assumptions, and make sure inclusion and fairness aren't afterthoughts. They may sit in compliance, finance, legal, or just be the trusted team member everyone knows will speak up.

The Experimenter

Curious. Scrappy. Doesn't wait for perfection. This person will test tools, break things, and bring back insights. They may not have a formal innovation role, but they're the ones who are already using GenAI in their day job, even if no one asked them to. These are your real-world testers and early signal finders.

The Storyteller

Every new capability needs a new narrative. This person helps shape the why, and translates that into clear, human messaging that others can connect with. They might be in L&D, internal comms, marketing, or a people leader who just knows how to bring others along.

The Influencer

They're not necessarily the loudest. But people watch how they respond before deciding what they think. These credibility anchors shape team sentiment whether they know it or not. If they're curious and engaged, others will be too.

What makes this model work isn't its structure, it's its adaptability. You won't need every voice at every table all the time. But you need a plan for when to pull them in. Different use cases; recruitment, performance, engagement, will require different combinations of this team.

And what keeps this team powerful is clarity. Clarity on decision rights. Clarity on communication. Clarity on the shared commitment to lead responsibly.

Ask yourself:

1. Who are the people in your organization that others trust to try something new and tell the truth about it?

2. Who naturally bridges gaps between business, tech, and people?

3. Who already shapes your culture, not necessarily because they have "authority", but because they have credibility?

Start here. This is your Dream Team. They're already influencing your business, and now you're just giving them a seat at the table with AI.

Cultural Readiness: Preparing for the AI Mindset Shift

Organizational culture will have a bigger impact on AI success than any technology you choose. We've all seen brilliant ideas falter because organizations weren't culturally ready for them. Success depends on building trust, encouraging open dialogue about AI, and creating an environment where people feel secure enough to experiment and occasionally fail.

The best AI strategy will struggle if your team doesn't trust the technology, understand its purpose, or feel safe voicing their concerns.

Before diving into implementation, take a moment to reflect on your last major technology rollout or change management initiative. What went well? What resistance did you face? How did leadership support (or hinder) adoption?

Now, as you explore AI, here are key questions to assess your organization's readiness:

- **Innovation Mindset:** When new technologies or processes were introduced in the past, how did your organization respond? Were employees excited, hesitant, or resistant?
- **Data-Driven Decision Making:** Are your leaders comfortable relying on AI-generated insights, or do they default to intuition and past experience?
- **Continuous Learning:** Does your organization actively encourage learning and adaptation, or do new tools often feel like one-time rollouts with minimal follow-up?
- **Trust in Technology:** Is there general trust in new technology, or do employees tend to be skeptical, particularly around automation and AI?
- **Ethical Considerations:** Have ethical discussions been a core part of past tech implementations, or is this often an afterthought?

Your past experiences with technology adoption can offer powerful insights into how AI will be received. Addressing these cultural factors now can make the difference between a successful AI integration and a frustrating, underutilized investment.

Exercise:
Cultural Assessment
Imagine you've just announced an AI implementation with your HR team.

1. Write down the top 3 positive reactions you'd expect from your team?

2. Write down the top 3 concerns you'd expect to hear from your team.

This can give you insight into your cultural readiness and potential resistance points.

Bringing It All Together: Your AI Readiness Scorecard

Now that we've covered the key areas of AI readiness, it's time to bring it all together. Create a scorecard for your organization, rating each area (Data, Technical Infrastructure, Skills, and Culture).

Quick Assessment:

Rate your organization on each factor from 1 (Not at all) to 5 (Fully implemented):

Data Quality & Infrastructure					
We maintain accurate, up-to-date employee records in a centralized HRIS	1	2	3	4	5
Our HR data is consistently formatted and standardized across systems	1	2	3	4	5
We have clear data governance policies and procedures	1	2	3	4	5
Our HR systems can easily integrate with new tools	1	2	3	4	5
We regularly audit our data for accuracy and completeness	1	2	3	4	5

Data Types Available

Recruitment metrics (time to hire, cost per hire, source quality)	1	2	3	4	5
Performance data (reviews, ratings, goals)	1	2	3	4	5
Learning & Development records	1	2	3	4	5
Compensation & benefits data	1	2	3	4	5
Employee engagement/survey data	1	2	3	4	5

Data Privacy & Security

We have clear data privacy policies	1	2	3	4	5
Employees understand how their data is used	1	2	3	4	5
We have data security protocols in place	1	2	3	4	5
We comply with relevant data protection regulation	1	2	3	4	5
We have a process for data access and permissions	1	2	3	4	5

Data Culture

HR team members are comfortable working with data	1	2	3	4	5
We regularly use data in decision making	1	2	3	4	5
Leaders trust and value data-driven insights	1	2	3	4	5
We have data literacy training programs	1	2	3	4	5
We have dedicated data analysts or similar roles	1	2	3	4	5

Total Points

After completing the assessment, total your scores to understand your organization's data readiness level.

- A score between **90-100** indicates advanced data maturity. Your organization has built a robust data foundation and is well-positioned to implement AI solutions. At this level, you can focus on optimizing your existing processes and exploring innovative AI applications.
- Scoring between **70-89** shows strong data readiness. While you have solid data practices in place, there are still some areas that need attention. You can begin implementing AI in your strongest areas while addressing specific gaps in your data infrastructure.
- Scoring **50-69** indicates you are in the developing stage. You have basic data infrastructure in place but need to strengthen key areas before launching major AI initiatives. Consider starting with pilot projects in your areas of strength while building up other capabilities.
- A score below **49** indicates you're in the early stages of your data journey. Your organization needs significant improvements in data management. Focus on building fundamental data practices before considering AI implementation. Start by establishing strong data governance and quality improvement processes.

This scorecard isn't about getting a perfect score, it's about honestly assessing where you are so you can plan your journey to AI readiness. Remember, every organization's path to AI will be unique. The goal is progress, not perfection.

Final Reflection

Based on your scorecard, what's the one area you need to focus on most urgently to improve your AI readiness? What's one concrete step you can take in the next week to start addressing this area?

Remember, assessing your AI readiness isn't a one time event. As you progress in your AI journey, keep revisiting these areas to ensure you're building on a solid foundation.

In our next section we'll look at how to build a compelling business case for AI in HR, turning your readiness into action. Get ready to make some waves!

3.2 Building a Business Case for AI in HR

You're standing in front of your company's executive team. The CFO is tapping her pen impatiently, the COO is checking his watch, and the CEO is giving you that "this better be good" look. You take a deep breath and begin your pitch for implementing your Project Plan for Implementing AI.

This scenario gives me flashbacks of bad memories. In one of my early in-house roles, I really stumbled over a presentation for a new HR strategy. I led with all the cool features of the software that got me excited, instead of focusing on the business impact. It was a hard lesson but one that transformed how I approach building business cases.

So, let's talk about how to craft a business case for AI in HR that will make your leadership team lean in, ask questions, and ultimately, give you that coveted green light.

Start with the Pain Points: The "Why" Behind AI

Here's the golden rule of building a business case: Don't lead with the technology. I know, I know, you're excited about all the shiny and cool things AI can do (and so am I). But trust me, leading with the sparkle is a surefire way to reinforce a false perception that HR only sees the shine and not the strategy! Leading with the larger business impact assures that your leaders understand you are leaning forward because of the business impact.

Start with the problems you're trying to solve. What are the pain points in your HR processes that are costing the company money, time, or talent?

For example:

- Are you losing top candidates because your recruitment process is too slow?

- Is employee turnover higher than industry standards, leading to constant rehiring and retraining costs?
- Are your learning and development programs failing to close critical skill gaps?
- How is a lack of connection impacting your employee hire to resignation ratio?

Paint a vivid picture of these challenges. Use real examples from your organization. I once started a proposal to change a years-long interview process with an anonymized story of a star candidate who chose a competitor because our hiring process took too long. You could have heard a pin drop in the room. Facts.

Remember, your goal here is to make the status quo more uncomfortable than the reality of making a change. And this change will require resources, attention, and commitment from all departments and levels. To get there you might need to get your c-suite squirming in their seats thinking, "We need to take action on this plan".

But here's a big caveat. Put a base outline plan together before the conversation, remember the old adage: Bring solutions, not problems.
And don't worry, you always have me to geek out about how magical it is.

Quantify the Current Costs: Speaking the Language of Finance

Once you've outlined the problems, it's time to put some dollar signs on them. This is where you'll grab the attention of your CFO.

Don't just say turnover is high. Provide clarity on numbers like, "Our current turnover rate of 20% is costing us approximately $5 million annually in recruitment and training costs." or "We're spending over 600 hours a year manually processing employee requests that could be handled more efficiently through automation."

Some areas to consider evaluating:

- Cost of unfilled positions (lost productivity)
- Recruitment costs (advertising, agency fees, time spent interviewing)
- Training and onboarding costs for new hires
- Cost of bad hires
- Lost productivity due to manual, time consuming HR processes

You don't need to be a finance expert to tell this story. You just need to speak in terms that frame your work as business value, and AI as the tool that helps reclaim it. If you're not comfortable with numbers, partner with someone from finance. I've found that finance partners often get excited about these projects when you involve them early in the process.

Paint the AI Enabled Future: From Pain to Gain

Now that you've set the stage with problems and costs, it's time to introduce AI as the solution. But remember, you're not selling AI tools. You're promoting outcomes.

Exercise:
Map Your AI Impact

For each HR challenge you identified, outline specific ways AI could help and quantify the expected impact. Here's how to build your analysis:

1. Current State

- Describe the challenge in detail (e.g., "Recruiters spend 15 hours per week screening resumes")
- Include current metrics where available
- Note the business impact of this challenge
- Document pain points for employees and candidates

2. Future State with AI

- Describe how AI would address this (e.g., "AI pre screens candidates based on job requirements")
- Project specific improvements: (e.g., time savings, cost reduction, quality improvement, satisfaction gains)
- Note which teams/roles would be most impacted

3. Transformation Journey

- What needs to change to achieve this future state?
- What obstacles might you face?
- What resources would you need?

4. Expected Impact

- What do you anticipate seeing in ROI wins?
- How will the organization and employees react/benefit?
- How will this reinforce or support driving business objectives?

By translating AI efficiency gains into business and financial-friendly metrics, you shift the conversation from "cool tech" to a business-critical investment. An investment that pays for itself in meaningful ways for employees and the organization.

Reflection Point:
Create these analyses for your top 3-5 challenges. They'll form the foundation of your business case and help you prioritize which AI solutions to pursue first.

This exercise helps you move from abstract benefits to concrete, measurable improvements that resonate with stakeholders. It also forces you to think through the full impact of AI implementation on your processes and people before you get in the room!

Be Realistic About Costs and Timelines: No Sugar Coating

Nothing will sink your business case faster than underestimating costs or overpromising on timelines. Be upfront about software, implementation, and training costs, as well as potential productivity dips during the transition.

Provide a realistic timeline for implementation and ROI. If possible, propose a phased approach to show quick wins while building towards larger goals. I learned the hard way as a VP of L & D many years ago. I once had a great business idea fall apart because I couldn't answer questions about ongoing maintenance costs, and once I asked those questions, it was clear that the ROI wasn't there in the long term. Don't let that be you.

Address the Risks: Show You've Thought It Through
Proactively discussing potential risks demonstrates maturity in your planning approach and builds credibility with stakeholders. Rather than seeing risk assessment as a negative, frame it as an opportunity to showcase your strategic thinking and problem-solving capabilities.

Key risks to address include:

- Data privacy and security concerns
- Employee resistance to new technology
- Potential bias in AI decision making
- Integration challenges with existing systems
- Resource constraints during implementation
- Vendor stability and customer support reliability

For each identified risk, develop a clear mitigation strategy. For example, addressing data privacy concerns might involve conducting thorough security audits, implementing enhanced encryption protocols, and establishing strict data governance policies. For employee resistance, your strategy could involve the early involvement of key stakeholders, continuous and comprehensive training programs, setting up a Slack or Teams channel for sharing successes, and clearly communicating how AI can enhance your teams' work.

The Secret Weapon: Emotion

Yes, you need the hard numbers and solid plans. But don't forget to tap into the emotional benefits:

- How will this make employees' work lives better?
- How will it help the company better serve its customers or fulfill its mission?
- How will it position the company as an innovative leader in the industry?

I once concluded a business case presentation by sharing anonymous quotes from employees about their frustrations with our current processes. It brought home the human impact of the changes we were proposing.

Bringing It All Together: Your Elevator Pitch

Finally, be prepared to summarize your entire business case in a few sentences. You never know when you'll have a chance encounter with a key decision-maker in the elevator or parking lot.

Here's a short script to get you started putting your idea together:

"Our *X current challenge* is costing us *$ quantified cost* annually. By implementing *X AI Solution* in our *X specific HR function*, we can expect *X expected outcome*, resulting in *X quantified benefit*. While there will be *X acknowledged risks/costs*, our research so far shows that this approach has *X proof point* for companies like ours with similar challenges. I've already gathered some key information from the vendor including: *X testimonials* and *X data security information*."

Remember, building a business case isn't just about getting approval. It's about setting realistic expectations and getting buy-in from key stakeholders. The more thorough and thoughtful your business case, the smoother your implementation is likely to be.

Exercise:
Pitching Your Idea

Now, it's your turn. Take a moment to draft your elevator pitch for AI in your HR department. In 2-3 sentences, how would you summarize the key problem, the AI solution, and the expected benefit to your CEO? Practice it, refine it, make it sing. Because you never know when you'll have that golden opportunity to plant the seed of transformation in your organization.

The next section covers how to evaluate and select AI tools and vendors. A critical step that can significantly impact your implementation success. We'll examine key criteria for assessment and provide a framework for making informed technology decisions.

3.3 Selecting the Right AI Tools and Vendors

Alright, you've done your homework. You've assessed your organization's AI readiness, built a compelling business case, and got the green light from leadership. Now comes one of the most crucial steps in leveraging AI: choosing the right tools and vendors.

Selecting an AI vendor for an HR project can be a bit daunting. The market is flooded with solutions, each promising to "revolutionize" our processes. In some ways it can feel like looking at the Cheesecake Factory® menu... both exciting and quite overwhelming.

So let's roll up our sleeves and dive into how to select AI tools and vendors that will truly deliver value to your organization. And don't worry. I've got a checklist that will make you feel like a pro when you're grilling those vendors!

Know What You Need: Defining Your Requirements

Before you start evaluating vendors you need to be clear about what you're looking for. It's like me heading out to Target®. If I don't have a plan I'll end up with a cart full of stuff I don't need, and $400 less in the bank.

Start by answering these questions:

- What specific HR processes are you looking to enhance with AI?
- What are your must-have features versus nice-to-haves?
- How should the AI solution integrate with your existing HR tech stack? (What AI functionality exists in your current tool stack?)
- What level of customization do you need?
- What's your budget, both for the initial implementation and ongoing costs?

Create a detailed requirements document based on these answers. This will be your North Star throughout the selection process. Consider what AI tools you might leverage.

You can always find an up-to-date list of AI tools for HR at peoplepower.ai

The HR Leader's AI Vendor Vetting Checklist

Now, here's the checklist I promised. Use this as a starting point to prepare for conversations when you're evaluating AI vendors, and to double check that you're covering all the crucial bases:

Data Security and Privacy	✓
Does they comply with relevant data protection regulations (e.g., GDPR, CCPA)?	
What data encryption methods do they use?	
How often do they conduct security audits?	
Do they have a clear data breach notification process?	
Can they provide a SOC 2 Type II report?	

Data Sources and Training	✓
Where does the vendor source their training data?	
How do they ensure the quality and relevance of their training data?	
Do they use synthetic data, and if so, how is it generated?	
How often is their AI model retrained or updated?	
Can they provide transparency on their data collection and usage practices?	

AI Model Transparency and Explainability	✓
Can the vendor explain how their AI makes decisions?	
Do they provide tools or reports to help understand the AI's decision making process?	
How do they handle "black box" scenarios where the AI's decision isn't clear?	

Bias and Fairness	✓
How does the vendor test for and mitigate bias in their AI models?	
Can they provide diversity and inclusion metrics for their training data?	
Do they offer features to monitor and report on potential bias in the AI's outputs?	
Have they had their AI audited for fairness by a third party?	

Customization and Scalability	✓
Can the AI be customized to your organization's specific needs?	
How easy is it to scale the solution as your organization grows?	
What level of support do they offer for customization and scaling?	

Integration Capabilities	✓
What APIs or integration tools do they offer?	
Have they successfully integrated with systems similar to yours in the past?	
Does the solution integrate with your existing HR systems?	

User Experience and Accessibility	✓
Does the solution offer multilingual support if needed?	
Is the tool accessible to users with disabilities?	
How intuitive is the user interface for both HR professionals and employees?	

Vendor Stability and Support	✓
How long has the vendor been in business?	
Can they provide case studies or references from similar organizations?	
What levels of customer support do they offer?	
What does their product roadmap look like?	

Performance Metrics and Reporting	✓
What key performance indicators (KPIs) does the tool track?	
How customizable are the reports?	
Can the system provide real-time analytics?	

Cost Structure	✓
What's included in the base price, and what are the additional costs?	
Are there any hidden fees (e.g., for data storage, additional users, etc.)?	
What's the pricing model (per user, per module, etc.)?	
Is there a clear ROI model?	

You can find a downloadable .pdf version of this checklist at peoplepower.ai

Remember, this checklist is a starting point. Feel free to add or modify items based on your organization's specific needs and concerns.

Beyond the Checklist: Trusting Your Gut

While this checklist is crucial, don't forget to also trust your instincts. Pay attention to how the vendor interacts with you during the selection process. Are they responsive to your questions? Do they seem genuinely interested in understanding your needs, or are they just trying to make a sale? Are they targeting responses to you directly, or are they targeting someone else in the room, such as IT?

I once walked away from an HRIS vendor after a few really exciting product demos because something felt off during our interactions. It turned out to be the right decision. I later heard they had major issues with customer support and had to go through a huge internal restructure that would have coincided with our implementation. Taking on new technology can be a challenge and I'm sure it would have been a nightmare beyond the normal implementation issues, with the company going through their own transition.

The Proof is in the Pilots and Trials

Whenever possible, do a pilot or trial run before committing to a full implementation. Even if they don't have a clear option for this on their website or through your early conversations, challenge them for this opportunity. This gives you a chance to see the AI in action in your specific context. Pay attention to:

- How well does it integrate with your existing systems?
- How do your team members react to it?
- Does it deliver the results promised in the sales pitch?

Involve Your Stakeholders... with a Caveat
Remember, you're not just choosing a tool for HR. You're selecting a solution that will impact multiple functions, workflows, and teams across your organization.

Involve key stakeholders in the selection process:

- IT for technical integration, data structure, and security
- Legal for compliance, privacy, and risk mitigation
- Finance for budgeting, cost modeling, and ROI validation
- End-users including HR team members, cross-functional partners, and employees for usability and adoption feedback

But I say that with a caveat: you're not seeking input to get permission. You're seeking expertise to make a more informed decision. HR leaders sometimes wait for sign-off or treat early resistance as a final answer.

. . .

Don't. Do. This.

These tools are central to how your function operates and how the business shows up for its people, and when it comes to HR systems and the technologies that shape the employee experience, HR must lead.

You understand the nuance, the pressure points, and the opportunities. So invite others into the process, but stay grounded in your expertise. The final decision may be cross-functional, but the vision should be yours.

The Long Game: Think About the Future

Finally, think beyond your immediate needs. Choose partners that aren't just solving today's problems, but that are also looking to the future and building technology that can adapt. Choose a vendor that's not just solving today's problems but is also innovating for tomorrow's challenges.

Look for vendors who:

- Have a clear product roadmap
- Invest heavily in Research & Development
- Are thought leaders in the AI and HR space

Remember, you are entering into a partnership. Choose a vendor you can grow with.

Selecting the right AI tools and vendors is a critical step in your AI journey. It requires careful consideration, thorough vetting, and a bit of vision. But with this checklist and these strategies in your toolkit, you'll be well-equipped to make a choice that will set your organization up for success.

3.4 Change Management and AI Adoption That Lasts

The success of your AI implementation depends far more on your people than on the technology itself. You can have the most advanced AI tool in the world but if your employees don't use it or trust it, it's all for naught.

Let's explore how to ensure your AI implementation doesn't just change your technology, but positively transforms your organization.

Begin with the 'Why'

Simon Sinek really plugged into an idea when he did his famous TedTalk, and beginning with the reason for the change makes sense for things like AI adoption as well. Before diving into the what or how of AI implementation, make sure everyone understands why it's happening. Communicate clearly how AI will improve work life, not just how it benefits the company. Address concerns about job displacement and the other fears we shared in Chapter 1 honestly and upfront.

Key steps:

- Develop a clear narrative about the need for AI
- Highlight specific pain points AI will address
- Share success stories from similar implementations

Identify and Empower Champions

Once your AI Dream Team is aligned, it's time to extend the influence. The real shift happens when early adopters begin to model new behaviors within their departments and bring others along. Not through authority, but through trust and credibility. These are your functional champions.

They're not always senior or technical. But they're the ones colleagues turn to for advice, watch for cues, and follow into new territory. In my experience, these informal leaders are often the difference between cautious curiosity and full-scale adoption.

To build a strong champions network, start by identifying natural connectors and respected voices across teams. Look for people who:

- Informally mentor others

- Show curiosity about improving processes
- Ask thoughtful questions about tech or transformation

Your champions should reflect a range of roles and perspectives. A junior recruiter may see opportunities a senior HRBP won't. A compensation analyst may spot edge cases others overlook. Diversity strengthens your implementation strategy and helps you anticipate resistance.

The key is to involve these champions early, before you've finalized your AI implementation plans. Give them a voice in selecting and configuring tools, designing training programs, and developing communication strategies. Their front-line insights will improve your plans and their early involvement creates authentic advocates for change.

Remember that champions need support to be effective. Provide them with:

- Comprehensive training on both the technical and strategic aspects of your AI tools
- Regular forums to share feedback and concerns
- Resources to help them support their colleagues
- Recognition for their role in driving change

Your champions network will evolve as implementation progresses. Some early champions may step back while new ones emerge. Stay flexible and keep nurturing these crucial relationships. They're often the difference between an AI initiative that transforms your organization and one that fails to gain traction.

Provide Ample Training and Support

Don't underestimate the learning curve that comes with new technology. Offer a variety of training options to cater to different learning styles and schedules.

Consider including various connection points and approaches, including:

- In-person workshops
- Online modules
- One-on-one coaching sessions
- Slack/Teams shared learning channels
- Regular 'AI office hours' for ongoing support

Remember, training isn't a one-time event. Plan for ongoing support and refresher sessions.

Success stories catalyze change but they need to be authentic and meaningful. Rather than focusing on dramatic transformations, look for the everyday improvements that demonstrate real value. This could be as straightforward as tracking time saved on routine tasks or measuring improvements in response times to employee queries.

When documenting and sharing successes, focus on concrete metrics and specific process improvements:

- Reduced time spent on administrative tasks
- Faster response rates to common HR queries
- More accurate candidate screening results
- Improved employee satisfaction with HR services

The key is to make these improvements tangible and relatable to different teams' day-to-day work.

Creating a Feedback Rich Environment

Implementation is just the beginning... the real measure of success comes from how your teams adapt, respond, and optimize AI tools over time. Without regular feedback loops, even the most promising tools risk falling flat, or worse, eroding trust with users who feel unheard.

A feedback-rich environment doesn't happen by accident. It requires intention, structure, and a culture where people know their input will lead to real change.

Here are a few ways to build that environment into your post-implementation plan:

- Schedule regular user group discussions to assess tool functionality, address friction points, and gather ideas for improvement

- Create anonymous channels through surveys, feedback portals, or even AI itself, to collect honest, unfiltered experiences from users
- Run structured check-ins with different stakeholder groups (managers, front-line staff, cross-functional teams) to capture diverse perspectives
- Establish clear escalation processes for technical issues or gaps in functionality, and ensure timely follow-up so users see action
- Share back what you've heard, what changes are being made, and where feedback is shaping future iterations

Feedback loops aren't just a best practice. They're what keep your tools useful, relevant, and trusted. The reality is that adoption rarely fails because the tool is broken. Adoption fails because the experience around it isn't responsive. Needs shift. Teams change. What worked in the pilot phase might feel clunky six months in. If you're not checking in regularly, you'll miss those moments when a small adjustment could prevent frustration or disengagement.

And it's not just about finding and fixing problems. Strong feedback systems also help you understand where AI tools are adding real value, so you can amplify what's working and build stronger cases for broader adoption.

So don't treat feedback as something to collect. Treat it as something to work with. That's how you ensure these tools keep delivering, not just in theory, but in practice.

Leadership in Practice

Leading AI adoption requires a balance of curiosity, credibility, and consistency. It's easy to be excited about what the tools can do, but real leadership is about staying grounded in what's actually useful and possible. A former HR leader of mine used to say, "Leadership sets the tone and HR models the behavior." That idea is more relevant than ever.

When it comes to AI, setting the tone means showing up with transparency and a willingness to experiment in public. It means naming both the potential and the limitations. It means acknowledging that adoption won't be perfect, and that not every use case will hit the mark on the first try. What matters more is how leaders navigate the learning curve. How they stay curious, keep the conversation open, and model thoughtful use of these tools inside their own teams.

Here are a few practical ways to lead AI adoption by example:

- Use AI tools in your own day-to-day work, and talk openly about how they are helping, or where they fall short
- Share both wins and missteps with your team to normalize experimentation and build psychological safety
- Show what it looks like to integrate AI into your existing workflows, rather than adding it as another task on the list

- Engage in ethical conversations out loud, not behind closed doors, so your team sees that responsibility is part of the process

When leaders model this kind of clarity and openness, it invites teams to step into AI adoption with confidence, not fear. It makes space for experimentation while reinforcing accountability, and it sets the foundation for thoughtful, long-term change.

Sustaining Change: The Long View

Sustainable AI adoption rarely follows a linear path. Different teams and individuals will adapt at different rates and that's normal. Focus on progress over perfection, and be prepared to adjust your approach based on real-world experience.

Key considerations for long-term success:

- Set realistic adoption timelines
- Monitor both quantitative and qualitative feedback
- Adjust training and support based on user needs
- Maintain open dialogue about impact and improvements
- Regularly share updates with your leadership team and employees

Like any transformation, success hinges on clear communication, structured support, and continuous iteration.

The most effective AI rollouts follow core change management principles: set clear expectations, provide the right training and tools, create multiple feedback loops, and ensure leadership models the behavior they want to see. Resistance isn't failure, but it will likely be something you hit upon through this adoption journey. The key is not just introducing AI, but embedding it in a way that feels natural, valuable, and aligned with how your teams work.

What is tough? That AI transformation can feel like both a marathon and a sprint. Keep momentum by celebrating small wins, adapting based on feedback, and reinforcing how AI enables people to work smarter, not harder.

Now that we've covered how to implement AI with clarity and confidence, it's time to step back and ask the harder questions: Are we doing this responsibly? Ethically? In a way that builds trust rather than erodes it?

Chapter 4

First Do No Harm:

Ethics and Responsibility in HR Tech

A s we've explored the potential of AI in HR throughout this book you've likely found yourself both excited by the possibilities and cautious about the implications. This is a reasonable and important response. While AI offers opportunities to enhance an organization's functions, it also presents unique challenges that we must address head-on.

While we've talked tactically in earlier chapters about what we can do to minimize overt and unconscious bias when using AI, in this section, we'll dive into the critical ethical considerations and best practices that should guide our implementation and use of AI in HR. We'll explore how to:

- Ensure fairness and reduce bias in AI systems
- Protect data privacy and security

- Promote transparency and explainability in AI decision-making
- Strike the right balance between AI efficiency and the human touch

As HR professionals, we're not just guardians of our organization's employees; we are the stewards of its values and ethical standards. The way we implement AI will significantly impact our workplace culture, employee trust, and ultimately, our organization's success.

Throughout this section we'll examine real-world scenarios, discuss practical strategies, and provide you with tools to navigate the complex ethical landscape of AI in HR. By the end, you'll be better equipped to leverage AI while upholding ethical standards in your HR practices.

Remember, ethical AI use in HR isn't just about compliance or risk mitigation, it's about building a foundation of trust, fairness and respect that will define the future of work in your organization.

Let's begin by exploring one of the most crucial aspects of ethical AI use: ensuring fairness and reducing bias.

4.1 Ensuring Fairness and Reducing Bias

As HR leaders, we've long stood at the forefront (oftentimes alone) in promoting fairness and reducing bias in our organizations. Now, as we integrate AI into our processes, this responsibility takes on new dimensions and increased importance.

The challenge of bias in AI isn't just a technical problem, it's a human one. Both issues deeply rooted in societal inequalities and historical disparities.

Understanding AI Bias in HR

Imagine you're reviewing the results of your new AI powered recruitment tool. You're excited about the efficiency it promises but something doesn't feel right. The candidates it's selecting seem oddly homogeneous. This scenario isn't just hypothetical —it's a reality many organizations have faced in the past few years.

Bias in AI doesn't exist in a vacuum. It's an extension and amplification of biases that exist in our society and workplaces. From recruitment and performance evaluations to promotion decisions and compensation, bias can creep in at every stage of the employee lifecycle.

One of the most well-known early warnings about AI bias came from a large tech company that trained its recruitment tool on ten years of hiring data. The data reflected patterns that favored male candidates, especially those from certain schools and job titles.

Without any explicit instruction, the AI learned to downgrade resumes that included terms like "women's," such as "women's chess club captain." This wasn't just a technical flaw, it was a mirror held up to the company's own systemic bias. And it made one thing painfully clear: if we don't audit what we teach these systems, they will inherit our blind spots and scale them. And if we don't train people with workarounds and the tools to report issues until the systems improve, we will be dealing with a lot more challenges.

This real world example underscores the critical need for vigilance in implementing AI in HR processes. When we introduce AI without careful consideration, we risk automating and scaling these biases, potentially widening existing gaps.

Key Sources of Bias in AI:

- **Historical data that reflects real-world inequality:** AI systems are trained on existing data, which often includes patterns shaped by historical bias and systemic discrimination. If past hiring practices, credit approvals, healthcare decisions, or legal outcomes were biased, the AI model will absorb those patterns and replicate them in its predictions or recommendations. Without intervention, the model learns to treat inequity as normal. *In HR, this is especially dangerous because it can quietly reinforce legacy decisions we're actively trying to change.*

- **Underrepresentation in training datasets:** When certain groups are underrepresented in the data, whether by race, gender, age, disability status, socioeconomic background, or geography, the model has fewer examples to learn from. This can lead to inaccurate predictions, weaker performance for those populations, and outcomes that reinforce inequality. Lack of diversity in the data almost always leads to lack of equity in the results. *This is one of the reasons I care so deeply about representation in both the data and the people building these systems. If we don't show up in the process, we won't show up in the outcomes.*

- **Human labeling and decision-making used as training input:** Many AI models are trained using data labeled by humans, or are designed to mimic human decision-making. But human decisions often contain bias, whether conscious or unconscious. If a model is trained on hiring decisions, loan approvals, or criminal justice outcomes shaped by flawed human judgment, it will learn those same patterns of bias and embed them in its logic. *This one's particularly tricky because it feels like progress. But if we're just digitizing bad habits, we're not moving forward... we're just amplifying the wrong behavior faster.*

- **Algorithm design that prioritizes accuracy over fairness:** Even with good data, bias can be introduced in how the model is built. Algorithms often optimize for performance metrics like speed or accuracy without accounting for fairness or ethical impact.

Without deliberate choices about what the model should prioritize, such as equal outcomes across groups or explainability, bias can be hardcoded into the system. Design decisions that seem neutral can have unequal consequences when deployed at scale. *One thing I've learned: just because something works well doesn't mean it's working fairly. We have to ask better questions during design, not just after things go wrong.*

- **Incomplete or context-blind data inputs:** AI models often lack access to the full context surrounding a decision. For example, performance evaluations might reflect workplace dynamics shaped by bias or structural disadvantage, but the model only sees the numerical ratings. Stripping data of human nuance can result in models that misinterpret or overgeneralize. *If we don't bring context back into the conversation, we end up making data-driven decisions that lack depth or empathy.*

- **Proxy variables that reinforce bias:** Even when sensitive characteristics like race or gender are excluded from a dataset, AI can still learn bias through proxy variables, things like: zip code, school attended, job title, or even email patterns. These proxies may strongly correlate with protected attributes, leading to biased outcomes even when the bias appears hidden. *I've seen this happen unintentionally in HR tools that seem "clean," but are quietly reproducing privilege. It's subtle, but it's real.*

- **Bias introduced during feature selection or engineering:** The way developers decide what information to include or exclude in a model (called "feature engineering") can introduce bias unintentionally. For example, choosing to weigh punctuality in attendance systems may disadvantage those managing caregiving responsibilities or dealing with accessibility challenges. *If HR isn't part of the build process, these signals can slip in without anyone asking what they really mean or who they might disadvantage.*

- **Lack of representative user feedback during model training:** When only certain users contribute feedback during early tool development or piloting, the resulting model can be skewed toward their expectations, language, or behaviors. If feedback is mostly coming from one region, team, or demographic, the model may fail to generalize appropriately across broader populations. *This is why I'm so bullish for including women and underrepresented experts in AI conversations. We need more voices, with more visibility if we want to ensure that future users of AI have a chance at more equitable and ethical tools.*

The Power of Diversity in AI Integrations

Reducing AI bias starts long before a tool is deployed. It begins with the team building and implementing it. Diverse implementation teams across gender, race, background, and lived experience are more likely to question assumptions, test for fairness, and flag blind spots. If the team building your system doesn't reflect the people it's meant to serve, you're more likely to build bias into the foundation.

Benefits of Diverse AI Development Teams

- More likely to identify potential biases that might otherwise go unnoticed
- Better equipped to anticipate and solve problems affecting a wide range of users
- More likely to design solutions with inclusivity in mind from the start
- More inclined to question data sources and consider a wider range of factors

As HR leaders with a unique opportunity to drive this change, we can actively seek out highly qualified diverse candidates for AI and data science roles, foster an inclusive workplace culture where diverse voices are heard and valued, and invest in programs that help underrepresented groups develop AI and data science skills.

Reflection Point: For those of you who have an "AI committee"/ "Dream Team" or similar group overseeing AI initiatives in your organization, take a moment to consider:

- How many women are represented on the committee?

- How many other underrepresented groups are included?
- How many HR team members are part of the group?
- Who leads the integration efforts?

Your answers to these questions can provide valuable insights into the diversity of perspectives shaping AI implementation in your organization and may highlight areas for improvement.

Exercise:
Auditing Your AI Process

Let's explore a thought experiment to apply these concepts to your organization:

Step 1

Choose an HR process in your organization that uses or could use AI (e.g., performance management, onboarding, L&D, benefits and compensation, engagement).

Step 2

Create three columns and list the following:

Process	Human	AI

Step 3

Map out each step of the process in column 1, identify where human decisions are made in column 2, and where AI plays or could play a role in column 3.

For each step, put on your "bias detective" hat:

- What potential biases could exist in the data available?
- How might the AI amplify existing biases?
- Are diverse perspectives involved in overseeing this process?

Step 4:

For each of the columns develop a bias mitigation review. Include the following questions in your assessment.

- How can you clean or balance the data used?
- What fairness constraints could you implement?
- How will you ensure ongoing monitoring and adjustment?
- Plan for transparency and human oversight:
- How will you explain AI decisions to affected employees?
- At what points should human judgment override AI recommendations?

The Path Forward: A Continuous Journey

Ensuring fairness and reducing bias in AI is not a one-time effort. Fairness is an ongoing commitment. While building a perfectly unbiased system may be impossible, that doesn't let us off the hook. What we can do is shape systems that improve over time, reflect our values, and extend opportunities, not limit them.

As HR leaders, we are uniquely positioned to lead this effort. By advocating for diverse teams, interrogating data sources, and designing inclusive processes from the start, we shift AI from a risk to a resource.

Bias won't vanish on its own. But when we show up with clarity, accountability, and curiosity, we can make sure the systems we adopt reflect the workplaces we want to build... not the ones we're trying to evolve from.

4.2 Data Privacy and Security

AI gives HR the power to understand, predict, and respond to employee needs like never before. But that power comes with responsibility, and risk. The data we hold about our employees is among the most sensitive in any organization: performance records, health information, compensation history, and even biometric or behavioral data. When AI enters the picture, that data isn't just stored, it can be analyzed, shared, interpreted, and sometimes acted on without a human in the loop.

This raises the stakes. A privacy failure isn't just a compliance issue. It's a trust-breaking event. In this section, we'll explore how to build systems and cultures that protect employee data while enabling responsible innovation.

The Data Privacy Landscape in HR

Reflect for a moment on the breadth of information we hold about our employees: personal details, financial information, performance records, health data, and sometimes even biometric information. Now, imagine if this data is processed by AI systems, potentially shared with third-party vendors, or stored in cloud platforms. It's a scenario that keeps me up at night when I consider the push to leverage AI without the training to ensure safety.

The stakes are high. A data breach or misuse of AI could lead to severe consequences including a loss of trust, repetitional damage, and financial and legal consequences.

Key Data Privacy Considerations in AI driven HR

Collection: What data are we gathering and is it truly necessary?

Storage: How and where is data stored? Is it properly secured?

Processing: How is AI using this data? Are we maintaining transparency?

Sharing: Are we sharing data with third parties? How is it protected?

Retention: How long are we keeping data? Do we have

a clear deletion policy (and do we have SOPs to keep up with it)?

Exercise:
Auditing Your AI Data Practices

When it comes to AI in HR, we all understand that privacy is not a compliance checkbox. It's a serious responsibility for every single person in our department (and those outside with access). Use this exercise to take a hard look at how employee data is being handled in your organization today. Think of it as a health check for your systems, policies, and assumptions.

Choose a process where employee data is actively being used. This could be performance management, learning personalization, engagement analysis, or internal communications. Then, work through the following areas of consideration:

1. Data Collection

- What data are we collecting as part of this process?
- Is all of it truly necessary to achieve the intended outcome?
- Are we collecting any data simply because we can?
- Have employees been informed about what data is being collected and why?

2. Data Storage

- Where is this data being stored: internally, with a vendor, or in the cloud?
- Who has access to it, and how is that access controlled?
- Are we encrypting sensitive data during storage and transfer?

3. Data Processing

- How is AI or automation interacting with this data?
- Can we clearly explain what the system is doing with the data to our employees?
- Are any sensitive categories such as health, ethnicity, or union affiliation being processed, even indirectly?

4. Data Sharing

- Are we sharing this data with any third-party tools, vendors, or partners?
- Do we have contracts in place that clearly define how the data will be handled, secured, and deleted?
- Could this sharing expose employees to risk they do not fully understand?

5. Data Retention

- How long are we keeping this data, and why?
- Do we have a clearly defined deletion policy, and are we following it?

- Is there any outdated or unnecessary data still sitting in our systems?

Reflection Point

After working through these questions, ask yourself:

1. If I were an employee, would I feel comfortable with how this data is being used?

2. Could I clearly explain our data handling practices to a skeptical employee or board member?

3. What is one immediate improvement I could champion, either in policy, process, or communication?

This exercise is not just about compliance. It is about earning trust through clarity, responsibility, and intention. And that starts with asking the right questions.

Navigating the Regulatory Maze

The regulatory landscape for data privacy is complex and ever evolving. It is important to stay aware of changes as they happen quickly and will have an impact on the future of your experience with AI. Here are some key regulations that impact our AI initiatives as of the publishing of this book:

- **EU AI Act** (2024): First comprehensive AI regulation globally. Classifies HR and recruitment AI systems as "high risk," requiring human oversight, transparency, and extensive documentation.

- **GDPR (General Data Protection Regulation)**: EU's data protection framework that includes specific provisions about automated decision making and profiling.
- **New York City Local Law 144**: Requires bias audits of automated employment decision tools and mandates candidate notification about AI use in hiring.
- **Illinois Artificial Intelligence Video Interview Act**: Requires consent and transparency when using AI analysis in video interviews.
- **CCPA/CPRA (California Privacy Rights Act)**: Enhanced privacy law that includes automated decision making provisions and employee data rights.
- **Colorado Privacy Act (CPA)**: Includes specific requirements for automated decision making systems, effective 2024.
- **State Level AI Regulations**: Growing number of states implementing AI oversight:
  - Virginia's AI Bill (2024)
  - Connecticut's AI Bill (2024)
  - More states developing similar legislation
- **HIPAA**: Remains relevant for health related employee data in the US.
- **Industry Specific Regulations**:
  - Financial services (SEC AI disclosure requirements)

- Healthcare AI guidelines
- Federal contractor requirements for AI use

The regulations for AI in HR are also rapidly changing. While this list captures major current regulations as of the publishing of this book, new laws and guidelines are being developed regularly. Staying informed through HR organizations, newsletters, law alerts and your legal counsel can help you stay current on requirements affecting your states of business and industry changes.

Strategies for Data Privacy and Security

1. **Data Minimization**
   - Collect only the data necessary for specific purposes
   - Regularly audit and delete unnecessary data
2. **Privacy by Design**
   - Incorporate privacy considerations from the outset of AI projects
   - Use techniques like differential privacy to protect individual data
3. **Robust Security Measures**
   - Implement strong encryption for data at rest and in transit
   - Use multi-factor authentication for access to AI systems
4. **Vendor Management**

- Thoroughly vet AI vendors for their privacy and security practices
- Ensure clear data protection agreements are in place

5. **Employee Consent and Transparency**
   - Clearly communicate how AI will use employee data
   - Obtain explicit consent for AI processing where required

6. **Data Governance Framework**
   - Establish clear roles and responsibilities for data management
   - Create and enforce policies for data access, use, and sharing

7. **Regular Audits and Impact Assessments**
   - Conduct Data Protection Impact Assessments (DPIAs) for high risk AI systems
   - Regularly audit AI systems for privacy compliance

8. **Incident Response Plan**
   - Develop and regularly test a data breach response plan
   - Ensure clear communication protocols in case of a privacy incident

Balancing Innovation and Privacy

It's crucial to remember that privacy protection and AI innovation are not mutually exclusive. In fact, robust privacy practices can foster trust and encourage employees to engage more fully with AI driven HR initiatives.

Case Study

Consider the following; a multinational corporation wanted to modernize its performance management process by implementing an AI-driven system. The goal was to provide employees and managers with more consistent, data-backed insights into performance trends, skill development, and areas for growth. At the same time, they wanted a shorter and less manual process. The HR team recognized early on that without transparency, clear governance, and leadership buy-in, they could end up with skepticism, disengagement, and even resistance.

The Challenge: Trust, Compliance, and Employee Concerns

As the company prepared for implementation, several concerns surfaced from employees and stakeholders:

- Transparency: Would employees understand how AI-generated insights were being used?
- Fairness: Would AI introduce biases or reinforce existing inequalities in performance evaluations?
- Data Privacy: How would sensitive performance data be stored, accessed, and protected?
- Employee Autonomy: Would AI recommendations dictate performance outcomes, or would employees have control over how their data was used?

Recognizing these concerns, HR and the leadership team decided to take a high communication and heavy human-centered approach to this new process, with a goal of ensuring that employees felt empowered rather than monitored.

The Approach: A Transparent, Ethical AI Rollout
Instead of deploying the AI system as a black box, where employees had little insight into how their data was analyzed, the company built trust through three key strategies.

1. **Full transparency in data use**—Employees were given clear, accessible explanations of what data the AI system analyzed, how insights were generated, and what managers would see.
   - AI-generated reports included explanations of the reasoning behind recommendations, ensuring that employees understood how insights were formed.
   - A dedicated AI Ethics Committee was established to oversee the fairness, accuracy, and accountability of AI-driven performance insights.
2. **Employee access and control**—Employees had the ability to review, correct, and challenge AI-generated insights about their performance.
   - AI recommendations were positioned as advisory, not definitive, ensuring that human judgment remained central to all performance decisions.
   - The company created a feedback loop where employees could flag concerns, suggest improvements, and report any perceived inaccuracies in AI-generated data.

3. **Strong security and privacy measures—**
   Performance data was encrypted, access was restricted to authorized personnel only, and clear policies were in place to prevent misuse.
   - Employees were informed about how long their data would be stored and had the option to request data removal after a set period.
   - A compliance team ensured that AI use aligned with their global privacy policy.

By proactively addressing these considerations, the company aimed to align AI adoption with both business objectives and ethical best practices. The outcome would largely depend on how well leadership communicated expectations, involved employees in the process, and maintained oversight of AI-driven decision-making.

Rather than viewing AI as a monitoring tool, employees saw it as a support system, one that helped them track their progress, set personalized goals, and prepare for career discussions with confidence.

This hypothetical case study demonstrates that AI adoption is not just about the technology, it's about the strategy behind its implementation. Organizations that prioritize transparency, fairness, and employee control can successfully integrate AI in ways that drive both business outcomes and workforce trust.

Over Communicate Change

When introducing any new process within your organization, communication is critical. When integrating AI tools into your organization, over communication is essential. I've talked with so many companies that are relying on osmosis to communicate change.

Employees, managers and functional departments will have questions, concerns, and assumptions about how AI works and what it means for their roles. Without clear, ongoing communication, misunderstandings can quickly turn into resistance.

A single announcement or training session is not enough. Employees and organizations need as many methods of communication as there are methods of adult learning. Multiple touchpoints, such as FAQs, live Q&A sessions, manager briefings, and hands-on demonstrations to reinforce key messages.

Over communication also helps prevent uncertainty and speculation. If employees don't know how AI is being used, they may assume the worst, that it's monitoring them unfairly or making decisions without human oversight. Repeating AI's purpose, limitations, and safeguards ensures employees feel informed and confident in the system.

In change management, if it feels like you're repeating yourself, you're likely communicating just enough.

Reflection Point

Think about your organization's current or planned AI initiatives.

- How transparent are you about data collection and use?
- Do employees have a clear understanding of how their data is being used in AI systems?
- What steps could you take to enhance privacy protections while still achieving your AI goals?

The Path Forward: Building Trust Through Privacy

As we move toward the world of integrating AI, let's remember that our role is to innovate responsibly. By prioritizing data privacy and security we're complying with regulations and building a foundation of trust with our employees.

Since the earliest days of HR, back when we were "personnel," being a great HR leader meant being a great data steward. With AI, this becomes even more critical. However, it is about striking the right balance between leveraging data for insights and respecting individual privacy. It's a challenge certainly, but one that has the potential to lead to immense rewards in terms of employee trust, organizational reputation, and ethical leadership.

4.3 Transparency and Explainability in AI Decision Making

We're navigating a new landscape where AI will become an integral part of our decision making processes. From hiring recommendations to engagement insights, AI systems are influencing how people are evaluated, promoted, and supported.

This shift introduces complex challenges, particularly around transparency and explainability. Let's break this down and explore why it's so crucial for us to get this right.

Without transparency, employees and leaders are left guessing about how decisions are being made. Without explainability, you lose the ability to defend, improve, or even understand the logic behind the outcomes AI is producing. If we don't get this part right, trust erodes quickly, and so does the confidence and credibility of HR's role in guiding the ethical use of AI across the organization.

Understanding Transparency and Explainability
First, let's clarify what we mean by these terms in the context of HR.

Transparency in AI refers to the clear and intentional communication about how AI is being used. It's about answering the "what, when, and who" questions: what data is being used, when AI is involved in a process, and who is responsible for the system's output. Transparency ensures that all stakeholders understand how AI fits into decision making, even if they're not technical experts.

Key elements include:

- What data sources are being used
- When AI is being used versus human decision making
- Who oversees and is accountable for the system
- Which processes involve AI
- What general capabilities and limitations exist

Think of the above as an easy checklist for how to prepare your organization for a new AI tool or process.

Explainable AI (XAI) is the ability to understand and articulate the specific reasoning behind an AI system's output or recommendations. While transparency focuses on visibility into when and where AI is used, explainability digs deeper. It's about unpacking the logic, inputs, and reasoning behind each output.

This matters because in HR, the decisions we influence: who gets hired, promoted, flagged for development, or exited, are high-stakes and deeply personal. If an employee or candidate asks, "Why wasn't I selected?" or "What made this person stand out?" you need to be able to answer with more than "The system said so."

Explainability turns AI from a black box into a conversation partner. It gives HR professionals the ability to interrogate results, catch potential bias, and build trust in the tools we use.

Key elements include:

- Which specific factors influenced a decision
- How heavily each factor was weighted
- What logical steps the AI followed
- What confidence level the AI had in its decision
- What alternative outcomes were considered

Generative AI and Explainability

One important thing to note is that Generative AI tools are not explainable in the way explainability is defined above for responsible AI governance. While generative AI tools like Chat-GPT, Claude, and others are not explainable in the traditional sense, they are far more than basic writing assistants. These platforms are becoming increasingly capable, supporting everything from custom GPTs/Assistant creation and interactive work-flows to full-scale program development, policy simulations, and tailored guidance tools.

Used well, they can streamline complex processes, accelerate innovation, and personalize experiences in ways we couldn't have imagined just a few years ago. But we still need to be clear-eyed about how and when we apply them. Because these systems are based on large-scale pattern prediction rather than traceable logic, they cannot show exactly how they arrived at a specific recommendation or decision.

That doesn't mean they lack value. It means they're not the right tool when your use case demands clear, auditable decision-making. If explainability is required, especially in areas like candidate evaluation, performance scoring, or policy enforcement, you need models or systems that can be interrogated and justified.

GenAI can be a powerful co-creator, but it's the right solution in all circumstances.

Real World Examples:
The purpose here is to show you the difference between these two concepts, not an exhaustive trip through these scenarios.

Recruitment: Using an AI system screening resumes for a software engineering role.

- *Transparency* would mean informing candidates that we use AI to conduct initial resume screening based on job requirements and experience.
- *Explainability* would mean that the AI system evaluated the candidate's resume, the job description, and the candidate's pre-hire Predictive Index™ profile results in making a recommendation. This candidate was rated highly because they have 5 years of Python experience (weighted at 40%), a computer science degree (30%), and demonstrated leadership experience (30%). Additionally, their years of experience reflect above the standard provided in the job description and

their PI^{TM} profile aligns as a 9/10. The system identified these factors as strong predictors of success based on historical hiring data. Alternative candidates were ranked lower due to less direct programming experience.

This distinction becomes crucial when you need to justify decisions or address concerns about AI bias in your HR processes.

Another example is using an AI powered system to analyze your annual employee engagement survey results. Seems like a no-brainer, since throughout your career, determining themes from engagement surveys often required a couch, spreadsheets, highlighters, and about 3 months' time.

AI feels like the silver bullet supporting quicker and easier insights. But when AI identifies 'Department A' as having "higher flight risk" than 'Department B', you need to be able to provide a clear rationale.

Lack of explainability could lead to:

- Underlying issues in work culture or management practices going unaddressed
- Difficulty justifying resource allocation for retention efforts to leadership
- Erosion of trust among employees if they feel unfairly labeled as "flight risks"

- Missed opportunities to identify and replicate successful engagement strategies across departments

This scenario illustrates why transparency and explainability aren't just nice-to-haves. They are essential for ethical, fair, and effective HR practices. Without understanding the 'why' behind the AI's assessment, we risk making misguided decisions that could negatively impact employee morale and retention efforts.

The Stakes: Why Getting This Right is Critical
Our AI systems should reflect our organization's values and ethical standards. Without transparency, we can't ensure this alignment.

1. **Maintaining Trust**: Employees and candidates need to trust that decisions affecting their careers are fair and unbiased. Unexplainable AI decisions can erode this trust quickly.
2. **Legal and Ethical Compliance**: Many jurisdictions are implementing or considering regulations around AI use in employment decisions. Without transparency and explainability we risk running afoul of these regulations.
3. **Continuous Improvement**: If we can't explain why our AI systems make certain decisions, how can we improve them or correct unintended biases?

When AI Gets It Wrong: Notable Examples

AI can provide powerful efficiencies and productivity gains, but it isn't perfect. And the issues can have an immediate trust breaking impact on an organization. Below is a small sample of some real-world risks and strategies to mitigate them.

Hallucinations and Falsifications

Hallucinations happen when AI systems generate false or misleading information with apparent confidence. They represent one of the most significant challenges in implementing GenAI tools. These aren't simple errors; they can have serious real world consequences.

- The legal industry has seen several high profile cases involving AI hallucinations. In 2023 two lawyers faced sanctions after submitting a legal brief containing fictitious case citations generated by ChatGPT. The AI confidently provided detailed but completely fabricated court cases, leading to professional embarrassment and potential disciplinary action.
- Similar incidents have occurred in HR contexts. A tech company's recruiting team reported that their AI tool invented candidate qualifications and past employers that didn't exist.
- In another case, an AI powered employee handbook generator created policies that referenced non-existent labor laws, potentially exposing the company to liability.

Yes, this is scary stuff. Does this mean we should put aside the use of AI tools? I don't think so, but it is critical that we get really clear on what and how we evaluate the output or recommendations from the tools we choose.

Why Hallucinations Happen

Unlike human errors, AI hallucinations stem from how these systems process and generate information:

- They create responses based on pattern recognition rather than true understanding
- They can blend different pieces of information in ways that seem logical but are false, also known as "making up the source"
- They tend to prioritize providing a complete answer over admitting uncertainty

Practical Prevention Strategies

1. Use structured prompts that instruct your AI tools to "only respond based on verified sources," or "cite specific company documents," this lowers the risk of made-up content.
2. Create standard operating procedures (SOPs) for when and how AI-generated outputs must be reviewed by a human before use, especially in employee-facing materials.
3. Use "sandbox" environments for testing prompts before pushing them into live workflows. Have your

team test for particularly challenging cases, inaccuracies, and tone mismatches.

4. Train staff to recognize signs of hallucinations (overconfidence, vague sources, inconsistent facts), and establish a checklist for validating output in critical use cases like policies, contracts, or evaluations.

5. Train your team to recognize "confident wrongness," which happens when AI sounds certain, even when it's completely off base.

Bias in Outputs

AI bias is one of the biggest concerns in HR, particularly in hiring and performance evaluations. You've likely heard of some of the more media heavy examples in recruitment. In one case, a company implemented an AI-powered recruiting system trained on past hiring data. As they started to see changes in their candidate pool, they realized that the system appeared to be prioritizing male candidates over equally qualified female applicants. The AI had learned patterns from previous hiring decisions, which reflected historical biases, and it continued to reinforce them.

Does this mean AI should be avoided in hiring and HR decisions? No, but it does mean that companies must be intentional in how they train and monitor AI systems to prevent bias from creeping into decision-making.

Why Bias Happens in GenAI

- The large language models (LLMs) powering many GenAI tools are trained on massive datasets, often scraped from the internet, which can include biased, outdated, or harmful content. These biases become embedded in the model's outputs unless actively addressed.
- The people designing, training, and fine-tuning these systems, whether vendors, data scientists, or in-house developers, and they bring their own assumptions to the table. Without intentional effort, those assumptions can shape what the AI learns and how it behaves.
- Most AI systems are built to optimize for efficiency or pattern recognition, not fairness. If fairness isn't built in from the start, it usually isn't there.
- Without diverse teams reviewing training data, testing outcomes, and auditing performance, bias becomes systemic, and HR ends up scaling inequity instead of solving for it.

Practical Prevention Strategies

1. Regularly audit AI decisions for bias by analyzing hiring, promotion, and evaluation patterns.
2. Train your team to look out for diverse and representative outputs to reduce systemic bias. Also train everyone in your organization to give feedback to GenAI tools (especially if they are using free versions) to let them know the output is false. Using the thumbs

down icon in most tools, or just instructing tools that they are wrong is good practice.to provide input on good and bad output.

3. Implement human oversight and auditing in AI-assisted decision-making to ensure fairness.

4. Use bias-detection tools that help identify and correct skewed AI recommendations.

Lack of Context Awareness

Just as humans may lack intuition, AI does as well, and in high-stakes workplace scenarios, that gap can be costly. AI systems process language based on patterns, not lived experience. Without proper guardrails, this can lead to responses that are technically accurate but contextually tone-deaf... or worse, completely wrong.

One example of this was with a company where we implemented an AI-powered HR chatbot to streamline employee questions about leave policies. It seemed like a win; fewer emails, faster responses. But during testing when employees asked about "maternity leave," the chatbot responded with information about generic unpaid leave, completely missing the company's actual paid parental leave policy. For expectant parents already navigating complex emotions, this would have been both frustrating and dismissive, and had we not caught it during out pre-launch test, it could have had a major impact on trust in the HR Team.

This isn't an isolated risk. AI tools, if not well trained and monitored, may offer irrelevant, outdated, or even misleading responses in areas like:

- Mental health accommodations
- Return-to-work policies
- Workplace safety incidents
- Cultural or religious observance guidelines

Why AI Struggles with Context

- It relies on language patterns, not lived experience. AI doesn't "understand" the difference between legal compliance and employee reassurance, it recognizes which elements in a response often appear together.
- It cannot infer tone, culture, or emotional nuance. What feels empathetic in one workplace might feel invasive in another. AI doesn't know the difference, unless you train it.
- It responds based on general data unless directed otherwise. Off-the-shelf models default to public sources or generic policy templates unless grounded in your actual organization's documents.

Practical Prevention Strategies

1. Train your Custom AI tools on internal content, not just public data. Feed it actual HR FAQs, Slack threads, benefits PDFs, and onboarding guides to anchor responses in your organizational reality.

2. Design fallback protocols for nuance-heavy queries. When a question involves leave, accommodations, conflict, or feedback, your system should flag it for human follow-up or direct users to live support.

3. Use prompt templates that reinforce context. For example: "Answer using only our company's HR handbook and avoid referencing external policies." This reduces hallucinations and misfires.

The Limits of AI Understanding

When employees don't understand how AI is being used in HR, trust erodes quickly. One company implemented AI-driven productivity tracking but failed to clarify what data was being collected. Employees later discovered that their keystrokes and browser activity were monitored, leading to an internal backlash and accusations of surveillance.

Does this mean HR should avoid AI in sensitive areas? Not necessarily, but transparency is key to maintaining trust and compliance.

Why Limitation Issues Arise

- AI tools are often trained on large, generic datasets that don't reflect your organization's values, culture, or diversity, leading to misalignment and unintended consequences.
- Algorithms make decisions based on probability, not context as mentioned above. This can result in

"accurate outputs that still violate ethical norms, such as penalizing someone for gaps in employment without understanding the reason.

- Tools may infer things about employees, like burnout risk or engagement levels, without transparency, consent, or mechanisms for the employee to respond.
- Vendors often don't disclose how their models are trained, updated, or validated, leaving HR leaders without clear oversight or accountability. (Hint - we should be asking these questions of our vendors when they don't disclose)
- AI can operate invisibly in workflows, especially when embedded in platforms like ATS, L&D tools, or employee experience platforms making ethical review an afterthought instead of a design principle.

Practical Prevention Strategies

1. Require your vendors to disclose how their models are trained, what data is used, and how frequently models are tested for bias or ethical risk
2. Develop internal review processes for any AI tool that makes decisions or recommendations about employees, especially in performance, compensation, or wellness
3. Include diverse, cross-functional voices in the AI evaluation process (HR, DEI, Legal, front-line employees) to surface blind spots early

4. Ensure every tool that touches employee data includes built-in ways for employees to understand, challenge, and correct AI-generated outputs

5. Treat every new tool like a new policy: would you be comfortable explaining it to your most skeptical employee? If not, rethink it

Keeping AI Honest: Guidelines for Smarter Oversight

1. Implement the "Trust but Verify" Rule

As you begin integrating AI tools into your daily work, it's critical to keep in mind that we need to maintain informed oversight. The "trust but verify" principle should guide how AI outputs are used, especially in high-stakes or externally facing work. Additionally, teams should be trained to thoroughly review all AI-generated content and avoid using it to explain or justify decisions they themselves don't understand. AI should never be treated as an unquestionable source of truth. Instead, establish clear internal guidelines for when and how human verification is required. For sensitive or business-critical outputs, develop validation checklists that teams can use to confirm factual accuracy, appropriateness, and alignment with organizational policies. Verification is not a lack of trust in the tool, it's a sign of leadership's commitment to responsible, reliable use.

- Train your teams to thoroughly review all outputs, and never use AI output to explain something team members aren't informed about.

- Never accept AI generated factual claims without verification
- Establish clear guidelines for what types of information require human verification
- Create checklists for validating AI outputs in critical processes

2. Set Clear Boundaries

The quality of AI output absolutely depends on the quality of the input. To get useful, trustworthy responses, we need to structure our prompts intentionally. Instead of asking vague, open-ended questions, it's far more effective to define the task, clarify the context, and reference specific documents or data sources. This helps the AI stay grounded in the right information and reduces the risk of hallucinations or overly generalized answers. When appropriate, prompts should also require the AI to cite sources or reference material to support its claims. These boundaries not only improve the reliability of the results but also make the process more auditable and transparent.

AI should support human judgment. Its power lies in augmenting expertise, and in helping our teams move faster without compromising rigor.

Remember: AI should augment human expertise, not replace critical thinking and verification procedures. The goal is to leverage AI's efficiency while maintaining accuracy and reliability through human oversight.

The Path Forward: Building a Culture of Responsible AI Use

As we integrate AI more deeply into our HR practices our goal should be to create a culture where AI is a trusted tool, not a magic trick. This means:

1. **Fostering Open Dialogue**: Encourage discussions about AI use across all levels of the organization.
2. **Continuous Learning**: Stay informed about AI developments and their implications for HR.
3. **Ethical Leadership**: Set the tone from the top that ethical AI use is a priority.
4. **Collaboration**: Work closely with IT, Legal, and other departments to ensure a holistic approach to AI implementation.

This journey towards transparent and explainable AI in HR isn't a sprint; it's a marathon. It requires ongoing commitment, adaptability, and a willingness to continuously learn and improve. But by taking these steps, we can ensure that our AI driven processes are not just efficient, but also fair, ethical, and aligned with the human centric values at the core of your organizations.

4.4 Balancing AI and Human Touch in HR

As we wrap up our discussion on ethical considerations in AI for HR, let's tackle one of the most crucial challenges: finding the right balance between AI efficiency and the irreplaceable human touch that's at the heart of HR.

The AI Human Relationship

AI has the potential to enhance what we do as HR leaders, and become the new power tool in our massive HR toolkit. It will not be a substitute for human judgment and empathy. In fact, if we are able to create a synergy where AI handles repetitive tasks and data analysis, freeing us up to focus on the uniquely human aspects of our role, we can actually tackle some of the biggest challenges our organizations face. Situations that time and manual process has prevented in the past.

Let's consider an example:

You are conducting annual performance reviews. AI could efficiently analyze performance data, attendance records, and project outcomes, providing an initial performance score. But it's the human manager who can contextualize this data, understanding the nuances of an employee's situation, their growth trajectory, and their potential. AI provides the data-driven foundation while humans provide crucial human interpretation and empathetic communication.

Areas Where AI Shines

AI can be incredibly valuable in certain HR functions:

- **Data Analysis**: AI can process vast amounts of HR data, identifying patterns and trends that might escape human notice.
- **Routine Tasks**: Things like scheduling interviews, answering common HR queries, or processing leave requests can be efficiently handled by AI.
- **Initial Screening**: In recruitment, AI can help shortlist candidates based on predefined criteria saving time for human recruiters.
- **Personalization**: AI can recommend tailored learning paths based on an employee's role, skills, and career aspirations.

Where the Human Touch is Irreplaceable

On the flip side, there are areas where the human touch is crucial:

- **Complex Decision Making**: When it comes to strategic decisions about organizational culture or talent development, human insight is key.
- **Conflict Resolution**: Navigating interpersonal conflicts requires empathy, emotional intelligence, and nuanced communication... all human strengths.
- **Leadership Development**: While AI can provide data on leadership potential, nurturing leaders requires human mentorship and guidance.

- **Ethical Considerations**: As we've discussed throughout this chapter, human oversight is crucial in ensuring AI is used ethically and aligns with organizational values.

Striking the Right Balance: A Practical Approach

So how do we find this balance? Here are some strategies to consider:

- **Define AI's Role Clearly**: For each process, delineate which aspects will be handled by AI and which require human input. Make these distinctions known to your team and the wider organization.
- **Emphasize the 'Augmented Intelligence' Approach**: Train your HR team to view AI as a tool that augments their capabilities, not as a replacement for their skills and judgment.
- **Prioritize Human Interaction for Sensitive Matters**: Ensure that sensitive conversations, like performance feedback or disciplinary actions, always involve human-to-human interaction.
- **Use AI to Inform, Not Dictate**: Treat AI outputs as valuable input but not as the final word. Always apply human judgment to AI generated insights.
- **Upskill Your Team**: Invest in training that helps your HR team work effectively with AI while also honing their uniquely human skills like emotional intelligence and critical thinking.

- **Regular Check-ins**: Periodically assess the impact of AI on your HR processes. Are you achieving the right balance? Are there areas where you need more human involvement, or where AI could be better utilized?

Looking Ahead: The Future of HR

As AI continues to evolve, our role as HR leaders will increasingly be about orchestrating this delicate dance between technology and human touch. We'll need to be tech savvy enough to leverage AI effectively, but also deeply in tune with the human aspects of our organizations.

The future of HR isn't about choosing between AI and human skills, it's about artfully combining both. By doing so, we can create HR practices that are not only more efficient but also more empathetic, fair, and aligned with our organizational values.

HR is about people. As we embrace AI, let's ensure it serves to enhance, not diminish, the human-centric nature of our profession. By striking the right balance we can create workplaces that are both high-tech and high-touch, leveraging the best of what AI and human capability have to offer.

Chapter 5

Looking Ahead

The Future of AI and the Future of You

Well, we've reached the final chapter of our journey through AI in HR. We've explored the foundations, grappled with ethical considerations, and examined practical applications. Now, let's turn our gaze to the horizon and consider what the future holds for us with AI.

This chapter examines three key areas that will shape how HR teams work with AI in the coming years:

1. **Continued Technology Evolution** We'll assess which emerging AI technologies are likely to have real impact in HR, separating practical advances from hype. This includes developments in automation, predictive analytics, and decision support tools.
2. **Professional Development** As AI reshapes HR work, new skills become essential. We'll outline

specific capabilities HR professionals need to develop, from data literacy to AI system evaluation.

3. **Organizational Readiness** Beyond individual skills, organizations need to evolve. We'll examine practical approaches to building AI capabilities while maintaining a focus on human needs and ethical considerations.

This discussion is about changes happening now that require thoughtful planning and action.

5.1 The AI Librarian Gets an Upgrade

Let's zoom out. The systems we're seeing now are just the beginning. Remember our trusty AI librarian from Chapter 1? Well imagine that librarian just got access to a whole new wing of the library, complete with cutting edge research papers, real time data streams, and a crystal ball (okay, maybe not the last one but you get the idea).

If we are to believe current media, AI is poised for dramatic transformation within the next 12-24 months, including the recent emergence of AI Agents and the ongoing development of Artificial General Intelligence (AGI). While current AI tools handle specific tasks, the future promises more sophisticated, interconnected systems that could fundamentally reshape how HR functions.

The Evolution of AI Agents

Today's AI assistants are just the beginning. What we're seeing now in tools that answer questions, summarize text, and handle repetitive requests, is rapidly evolving into something more powerful: AI agents. These are systems that can not only understand intent but also act on it across multiple steps, tools, and systems.

In HR, this changes the game. Rather than toggling between platforms, reconciling data, or manually pushing processes forward, AI agents can begin to operate like trusted colleagues. They could coordinate interview scheduling based on hiring velocity and team availability, automatically flag skills gaps from learning dashboards and performance systems, or even trigger stay interviews when early signs of disengagement appear in communication patterns.

Unlike simple chatbots or task-based tools, AI agents are designed to be proactive, not just reactive. They learn over time, adapt to your workflows, and integrate actions across disconnected systems. The result is not just task automation, but *decision support and execution*. This is what will make them central to how HR delivers strategic value in the future.

An example of how AI Agents could show up in the benefits and compensation space:

- Autonomously monitor and analyze global compensation trends
- Predict market shifts before they impact compensation strategies
- Identify subtle patterns in benefits utilization that suggest needed policy or strategy changes (or price fluctuations)
- Proactively suggest total rewards adjustments based on multiple factors
- Create dynamic compensation models that adapt to changing business conditions

These aren't isolated tools but interconnected systems that understand the relationship between different HR functions and business objectives.

The Future (and Hype) of AGI in HR

Artificial General Intelligence (AGI) is still pretty much a theory, but its potential impact on HR is worth serious discussion. Unlike today's specialized AI systems, AGI would operate with human-like reasoning across multiple domains, fundamentally changing how HR functions. If AGI becomes reality, here's how it could reshape the workplace.

1. **AI as the Ultimate HR Strategist**
   - Analyzing complex organizational dynamics to predict workforce needs
   - Understanding subtle factors that influence compensation effectiveness

- ○ Adapting benefits strategies based on emerging social and economic trends
2. **Smarter, Connected HR**
   - ○ Seamlessly connecting insights across all HR functions
   - ○ Understanding the broader business context of HR decisions
   - ○ Applying learnings from one area to improve others
3. **A Self-Learning HR Engine**
   - ○ Continuously updating its understanding of HR best practices
   - ○ Adapting to new regulations and compliance requirements
   - ○ Developing novel solutions to emerging HR challenges

Multi-Agent Systems and AI Swarms

In the next few years we will also likely see the rise of multi-agent systems or "agent swarms," where teams of autonomous AI agents work together to tackle complex tasks. These systems will likely:

- Orchestrate multiple specialized agents to solve high impact business challenges
- Handle end-to-end workflows through agent collaboration
- Develop "Chief of Staff" agents to oversee and coordinate other agents

Advanced AI Agents with Enhanced Autonomy

AI agents are predicted to become more sophisticated and capable. These agents will manage complex, real time tasks and adapt to ongoing changes such as shifts in consumer behavior or weather patterns. As these agents evolve, they will move beyond simple responses to actively executing and adapting in real time. Agents will:

- Transition from basic chatbots to advanced multi agent systems for enterprises.
- Develop natural voice capabilities to interact and act on customer requests.
- Create personalized AI experiences tailored to individual customers.

Multimodal AI Advancements

Already in place within several systems, multimodal AI models will likely become more sophisticated in processing and generating various types of data including text, images, audio, and video. This advancement will enable more intuitive and versatile AI applications, allowing for more natural interactions between humans and AI systems.

AI Driven Personalization at Scale

AI driven personalization is expected to reach new heights with algorithms becoming more sophisticated in understanding individual user preferences and behaviors. This will lead to highly tailored experiences across various platforms, from content recommendations to personalized product offerings.

Following the disruption and change of AI since the launch of ChatGPT in November of 2022 has been like drinking from a firehose. It comes fast and furious, and AI will continue to evolve rapidly, becoming more integrated into various aspects of business operations while also addressing current limitations and challenges. The focus is shifting from experimentation to practical, strategic applications that can deliver measurable business outcomes.

A Note of Realism

While the potential of AI agents and AGI, and other developments are exciting to consider, it's important to maintain perspective. The goal isn't to replace humans but to augment their capabilities with increasingly sophisticated tools. The future of HR will likely be a partnership between human judgment and artificial intelligence, each bringing unique strengths to the challenge of managing and developing the employee experience.

Exercise:
Future Gazing in Your Organization

Let's put on our futurist hats for a moment. Think about your organization and its current challenges. For each of the future trends we discussed:

Identify one specific way this technology could address a current pain point in your HR processes.

- What potential benefits could this bring to your organization?
- What concerns or challenges might you need to address to implement this technology?
- Who are our AI Partners in Crime to ensure that the technology changes are experienced across workflows throughout the organization?

In the next section we'll explore how we can upskill ourselves and our teams to thrive in this AI driven future. But before we do, take a moment to reflect on how far we've come. From being intimidated by AI to now envisioning its future applications.

5.2 Becoming AI Savvy Leaders

When I first started exploring AI in HR I felt like I was learning a new language. My prompts (once I learned they were called that, and not "googling AI") were clunky, but it was exciting... and a bit overwhelming. Now, looking at how far we've come, I'm amazed at the possibilities. But here's whatI always share with HR leaders and students:as AI evolves so must we. Let's talk about how we can stay ahead of the curve and become true AI savvy leaders in HR.

The Data Journey: From Spreadsheet Anxiety to Strategic Insight

I remember staring at my first Learning & Development dashboard in the early 2000s, feeling completely overwhelmed. The metrics were there. Course completion rates, training hours, and participant satisfaction scores, but translating them into meaningful business impact felt like I was in the matrix. Back then, analytics weren't a priority. We tracked attendance and smiled at positive feedback forms.

But the business world was changing. In one particularly memorable executive meeting, my CFO asked about the ROI of our new leadership program. I had feedback forms showing people loved it, but no data to prove business impact. It was clear that the happy feedback surveys were no longer the yardstick we'd be using and it changed my approach to HR data forever.

Today's AI tools make data analysis infinitely more accessible. They can automatically surface patterns and correlations that once required hours of manual analysis. But here's the key: you still need to understand enough about data to ask the right questions and critically evaluate the answers. Start with one area you're passionate about. Maybe it's retention patterns in high-performing teams or the relationship between learning programs and promotion rates. Let your curiosity guide your data literacy journey.

Beyond the Basics: Understanding AI's Role in HR

AI literacy isn't about becoming a technical expert. It's about understanding possibilities and limitations. Think of it like driving a car. You don't need to know how the engine works but you do need to understand what the vehicle can and can't do, how to operate it safely, and when it needs maintenance.

Each time you interact with AI tools in your daily work, be curious about how they make decisions.

- What data are they using?
- What assumptions are they making?
- What biases might be present?

This practical understanding will make you a more effective leader in an AI enhanced workplace.

Critical Thinking in an AI World

The true value of HR leaders in an AI powered future is not in processing information; AI will handle that. It will be in asking the questions that machines can't think to ask. If AI can help us predict our highest performers leaving despite high engagement scores, what can we do to build the conversation, connection and communication to prevent it?

These nuanced, context-dependent questions require human insight.

Exercise:
Personal AI Readiness Checklist
Let's do a quick self-assessment. Rate yourself on a scale of 1-5

(1 being "I need to work on this" and 5 being "I've got this down") on the following:

Personal AI Readiness Checklist					
I can explain basic AI concepts to non-technical colleagues	1	2	3	4	5
I'm comfortable reading and interpreting data visualizations	1	2	3	4	5
I understand the potential biases in AI systems and how to mitigate them	1	2	3	4	5
I can identify ethical concerns in AI applications	1	2	3	4	5
I have experience leading change management initiatives	1	2	3	4	5
I stay updated on emerging AI trends in HR	1	2	3	4	5
I can articulate the strategic value of AI in HR to senior leadership	1	2	3	4	5

How did you do? Don't worry if you didn't score 5's across the board. The goal is to continue to move up the scale. Identify your lowest scores and take a few moments to craft a plan to improve in those areas. Maybe it's taking an online course, reading more on the topic, or finding a mentor who's strong in that area.

Becoming AI savvy isn't a destination, it's a journey. And you're already well on your way! In our next section, we'll look at how to prepare your entire organization for this AI driven future. But for now, pat yourself on the back for how far you've come. From AI novice to AI advocate. You're taking control and on the right path!

5.3 You Got This: Leading the AI Revolution

Alright, we've talked about emerging trends and how to upskill ourselves. Now comes the big question: how does HR prepare an entire organization for an AI driven future? As HR leaders this is where we really get to shine.

Cultivate a Learning Culture: Curiosity is the New Competitive Advantage

First things first: we need to foster an environment where continuous learning is expected. In my experience, organizations that thrive in the AI era are those where everyone from the CEO to the recently hired intern is committed to learning and growth.

Here are a few ways to make this happen:

- Implement a learning platform to track and personalize learning paths. If you are a small business, this could be using a simple notion board or excel worksheet.
- Encourage cross-functional projects. This exposes people to different aspects of the business and helps

them see how new ideas and perspectives can be applied.
- Celebrate learning victories. When someone completes a course or applies a new skill, shout it from the rooftops (or at least in the company newsletter/Slack/Teams channel).

The goal is to make learning a habit and not a chore. As one of my mentors used to say, "The most dangerous thing you can do is to stop learning." But learning can't just be an individual priority, it needs to be a company-wide commitment. When organizations embed continuous learning into their culture, they don't just keep up with change... they drive it.

Develop an AI Strategy: Don't Just Adopt, Adapt

Having a clear AI strategy is crucial. Without it you risk ending up with a hodgepodge of AI tools that don't work together or align with your business goals.

Trust me, I've seen it happen, and it's not pretty.

Here's a simple framework I use:

- **Assess**: What are your current pain points? Where could AI make the biggest impact?
- **Align**: How does AI fit into your overall business strategy?
- **Plan**: What resources (budget, talent, data) do you need?

- **Implement**: Start small, learn, and scale.
- **Evaluate**: Regularly review and adjust your AI initiatives.

In 2024 I did some AI integration work with a small residential real estate organization. The CEO was very bullish about the potential of AI and mandated "We need to have everyone using AI yesterday." They ended up with disparate tools, limited adoption, and a lot of confusion across the organization. It ended up taking so long to unravel all of that work that could have been saved if there was a plan from the get-go. Don't let this be you!

Rethink Job Roles and Skills: Prepare for Jobs That Don't Exist Yet

The impact of AI on job roles requires thoughtful, proactive leadership from HR. While we may be skilled to oversee a variety of changes, from layoffs to acquisitions, AI's broad impact demands a new approach. An approach that balances honesty about coming changes with concrete support for transitions, particularly for roles that will become obsolete as AI improves.

Start by identifying roles that will see significant evolution:

- Positions where 40%+ of work involves routine data processing
- Administrative roles focused on document handling and basic analysis

- Jobs centered on pattern recognition and routine decision making
- Roles heavy in standardized customer service or information sharing

Building effective transition programs means starting before change becomes urgent. That begins with thoughtful assessment and development planning:

- How can we map current skills against future organizational needs?
- How can we create individual development plans with clear milestones?
- How do we identify transferable skills that align with emerging roles?
- What are realistic timelines for skill development?

For larger organizations, an internal skills marketplace has proven particularly effective for supporting role transitions. This approach allows employees to explore new opportunities while building capabilities the organization needs for the future. It reduces the risk of transition while maintaining engagement.

For smaller organizations, a full-scale internal skills marketplace may not be feasible, but the same principles can be applied in a more flexible, resource-conscious way. Instead of a formalized system, smaller teams can create personalized career pathways that help employees explore new roles and skills within the company while aligning with business needs.

Key strategies to support the transition might include:

- Cross-training and job rotation programs to help employees gain hands-on experience in different roles.
- One-on-one career conversations with leadership to identify growth opportunities and align skills with company needs.
- Access to external learning resources, including free or affordable online courses and industry certifications.
- Project-based learning and stretch assignments that allow employees to gain new experience without requiring a formal role change.
- Wellness and transition support, ensuring employees feel supported during career shifts, even in a leaner organization.

Smaller organizations have the advantage of agility, meaning they can customize learning and career development without the red tape of larger enterprises. The key is making growth opportunities visible, accessible, and integrated into the company culture.

Remember that successful transitions take time. While AI implementation might move quickly, people need space to process change, develop new skills, and make informed decisions about their futures. Your role is to provide both the tools and the time for meaningful career evolution.

Conclusion: HR's Role in Leading AI Adoption

As we close this book, I want you to know this: you are the right person and team for what is ahead! You are not only ready for the future of work. You're shaping it. Taking the time to learn more and build a plan to integrate AI into your teams and organizations isn't a one-time shift. It will be an ongoing evolution.

AI is a powerful tool but that's all it is... a set of tools. The real impact happens when you pair AI's capabilities with what makes us uniquely human: empathy, creativity, and strategic thinking.

With the insights you've gained and the strategies we've explored, you're well-equipped to lead the way.

As you move forward remember that AI's value comes from how we use it. Making organizations more efficient, effective, and, most importantly, human.

The future is bright and HR is at the forefront. Your expertise in people, your forward-thinking mindset, and your ethical leadership make you the ideal guide for this shift.

When you adopt AI thoughtfully, responsibly, and with a spirit of curiosity and innovation, you're leading the way into a new era of possibility. You are redefining HR and your role. With AI in your hands, you will transform work for the better.

Final Thoughts: AI Isn't Waiting, and Neither Are You

If you've made it this far, you're already leading.

You've asked hard questions. You've stayed curious when it would've been easier to shut the door. And you've leaned into a conversation that most people are still trying to avoid.

This work isn't easy. I know that. You're balancing complexity, emotion, pressure, and expectations... sometimes all in the same day. And now we're adding AI to the mix?

But here's what I need you to know:

You are not behind. You're not unqualified.

And you are absolutely capable of leading your team, your function, and your organization through what's next. You don't need to be a technologist. You need to be you—sharp, thoughtful, human-first, and clear on what good looks like.

So take what resonated.

Use what fits.

Adapt what doesn't.

And if you're wondering where to start? Bring these three questions into your next leadership conversation:

1. **Where are we making people work around broken systems?**
2. **What are we measuring just because it's easy, not because it matters?**
3. **How can we use AI to bring us closer to our people, not further away?**

Your intentionality to connect AI with improved people experience and business outcomes can be a force multiplier.

And you're already doing more than you realize.

You've got this. And I've got you.

Let's keep going.

Theresa Jesinstine

Acknowledgments

This book would not exist in its current form without the insight, encouragement, and thoughtful challenges of a few key people I want to thank from the heart.

To **Lynda Fraser**—Thank you for always bringing that steady big sister energy. Your support throughout this journey meant more than I can say. Your early edits were instrumental in helping me organize the chaos, make the ideas flow, and create something that could actually serve people. You've been in my corner since the beginning, and it shows.

To **Nadia Eran**—Your straightforward feedback, your clarity, and your willingness to tell me the truth (even when it was hard to hear) pushed this book to a deeper, sharper place. You helped me dig in and level up, and I'm so grateful you were willing to be part of the early process.

To the **TroopHR** and **Culture First** communities—Thank you for showing me what community really means. You've created spaces that don't just connect people, but uplift them.

You've shaped my thinking, strengthened my conviction, and reminded me again and again why this work matters.

To everyone who took time to read, review, reflect, or simply cheer me on, thank you. Your words, your presence, and your belief in this work carried me through more than you know.

About the Author

Theresa Fesinstine is a recognized leader at the intersection of HR and AI. With over 25 years of experience in HR leadership, Theresa has built a career rooted in operational excellence, talent development, and employee engagement.

As the Founder of peoplepower.ai, she is on a mission to flatten the AI learning curve for HR Leaders and Teams. Her work is driven by a deep belief that AI shouldn't be intimidating, it should be accessible, ethical, and actionable. She's received numerous honors for her contributions to AI thought leadership, including the Dextego AI Award and recognition as a PYN 50 Over 50 Women in Tech.

Theresa holds a certification in AI for Business Strategy from MIT and serves as an Adjunct Professor of AI for Business and HR Management at the City College of New York, where she helps prepare the next generation of business leaders to think strategically about technology and people.

She's a trusted advisor to AI-first startups, a mentor with All

Tech is Human, and an active contributor to professional communities like TroopHR and Culture First. Whether speaking onstage, writing, or consulting, her focus remains the same: helping people-first leaders embrace technology without losing the human touch.

What's Next?

If this book has done its job, you're no longer waiting for permission to lead the AI conversation in your organization. You're ready and already moving. But this isn't a one-and-done moment. The technology will evolve. So will the conversations. And so will you.

Here are a few meaningful next steps to stay connected, deepen your expertise, and lead with others who are building the future of HR responsibly.

Keep learning.
Explore additional resources and practical tools at peoplepower.ai, where you'll find curated templates, recommended tools, and evolving playbooks to help you implement what you've learned here.

Stay connected.
Subscribe to the newsletter to receive regular insights, new case studies, and examples from the field. No jargon. Just real stories and strategies from real teams doing the work.

Lead the conversation.
Invite others in your org to read this book. Use it to spark dialogue in leadership meetings, AI working groups, or team offsites. Use it as a map, but make it your own.

Join the community.
Change is easier when you're not doing it alone. Join the community on Linkedin at peoplepower.ai to meet other HR leaders and AI-curious professionals who are asking the same questions and experimenting with new answers.

Bring the conversation to your company.
If your leadership team or board is beginning to ask, "What do we do with AI?" you have a framework now. And if you need support facilitating those conversations, I'd be honored to help.

We are the stewards of the future of work. Let's lead it with curiosity, cautious optimism, and care.

www.ingramcontent.com/pod-product-compliance
Lightning Source LLC
Chambersburg PA
CBHW061749120626
46550CB00005B/1934